SINGER

SEWING REFERENCE LIBRARY®

More
Creative Sewing Ideas

Cy DeCosse Incorporated
Minnetonka, Minnesota

SINGER

SEWING REFERENCE LIBRARY®

More Creative Sewing Ideas

Contents

Introduction **7**

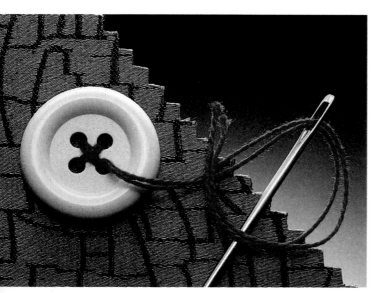

Creative Details **9**

Discovering Design
  Details 10
Copying Design
  Details 12
Couture Sleeve
  Detail 14

Creating Lace by
  Machine 20
Ruching 22

Creating Your Own Fabric **29**

Creating Hand-dyed
  Fabric 30
Tie-dyeing 36
Marbling Fabrics 41
Creative Lace 44
Creating Heirloom
  Fabric 48
Creating Special
  Effects 52

Surface Design
  & Embellishment 58
Piecing 60
Seminole Patchwork 62
Slashing 65
Appliqué, Embroidery
  & Beading 66
Adding Shine
  & Sparkle 68

Library of Congress
Cataloging-in-Publication Data

More creative sewing ideas.

  p. c.m. — (Singer sewing reference library)
Includes index.
ISBN 0-86573-276-0
ISBN 0-86573-277-9 (pbk.)
1. Sewing. 2. Needlework.
I. Cy DeCosse Incorporated.
II. Series.
TT705.M63   1992
646.2 — dc20   92-9272

Distributed by: Contemporary Books, Inc.
  Chicago, Illinois

CYDECOSSE INCORPORATED
Chairman: Cy DeCosse
President: James B. Maus
Executive Vice President: William B. Jones

MORE CREATIVE SEWING IDEAS
Created by: The Editors of Cy DeCosse
  Incorporated, in cooperation with the
  Sewing Education Department, Singer
  Sewing Company. Singer is a trademark
  of The Singer Company and is used
  under license.

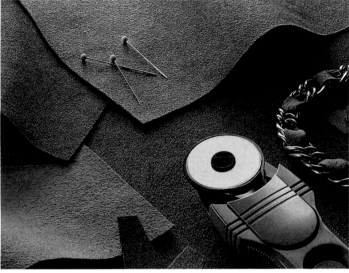

Fiber Art **71**

Color & Design for
  Quilting 72
English Smocking 76
Smocked Christmas
  Ornament 81

Rag Baskets 84
Rug Braiding 87
Hand Appliqué for
  Quilting 90

Creative Sewing Projects **95**

Creative Projects for
  You & Your Home 96
Handbag with Inset 98
Designer Belts 102
Scarves 104
Sew a Comforter Cover
  from Sheets 107
Bed Skirt with Clustered
  Gathers 111

Double-flange Pillow
  Sham 114
Slipcovers for Folding
  Chairs 119
Reverse Roll-up
  Shade 124

Executive Editor: Zoe A. Graul
Technical Editor: Rita C. Opseth
Project Manager: Deborah Bialik
Senior Art Director: Lisa Rosenthal
Art Directors: David Schelitzche, Brad
  Springer, Lori Swanson
Editor: Janice Cauley
Sample Supervisor: Carol Olson
Styling Director: Bobbette Destiche
Technical Photo Director: Bridget Haugh
Sewing Staff: Anne Cherry, Phyllis Galbraith,
  Kristi Kuhnau, Linda Neubauer, Carol
  Pilot, Sue Stein, Nancy Sundeen
Fabric Editor: Joanne Wawra
Photo Studio Managers: Cathleen Shannon,
  Rena Tassone
Photographers: Rex Irmen, Bill Linder,
  Mike Parker, Phil Aarestad, Paul Herda,
  Chuck Nields

*Director of Development Planning
  & Production:* Jim Bindas
Production Manager: Amelia Merz
Electronic Publishing Analyst: Joe Fahey
Production Staff: Carol Harvatin, Mike
  Schauer, Linda Schloegel, Nik Wogstad
Consultants: Sandra Betzina, Charlene
  Burningham, Roberta Carr, Clotilde,
  Patricia Cox, Betty L. Craig, Kathleen
  Ellingson, Amy Engman, Sandra Ericson,
  LaVonne J. Horner, Mev Jensen, Jules &
  Kaethe Kliot, Alice Lewis, Debra Millard
  Lunn, Adele Martinek, Linda McGehee,
  Ann Price, Marlys M. Riedesel, Donna
  Salyers, Jane Schneck, Sue Stein, Melanie
  Teig-Schwolert, Marilyn Tkachenko, Susan
  Voight-Reising, Nancy Ziemen
Contributors: B. Blumenthal & Co., Inc.;
  Braid-Aid; Clotilde; Coats & Clark Inc.;

Conso Products Company; Creative Fibers;
Crown Textile Company™; Dritz
Corporation; Dyno Merchandise
Corporation; EZ International; Ghee's®;
G-Street Fabrics; JHB International, Inc.;
Nancy's Notions, Ltd®; Olfa Products
Corporation; Paco Despacio, Buttonsmith;
Pellon Division, Freudenberg Nonwovens;
Scandia Down Shops; Sew-Art
International; The Singer Company;
Speed Stitch, Inc.; Streamline Industries,
Inc.; Swiss-Metrosene, Inc.; Tandy Leather
Co.; Thai Silks; Velcro USA, Inc.; Wm. E.
Wright Company; YLI Corporation
Printed on American paper by: Ringier
America, Inc. (1292)

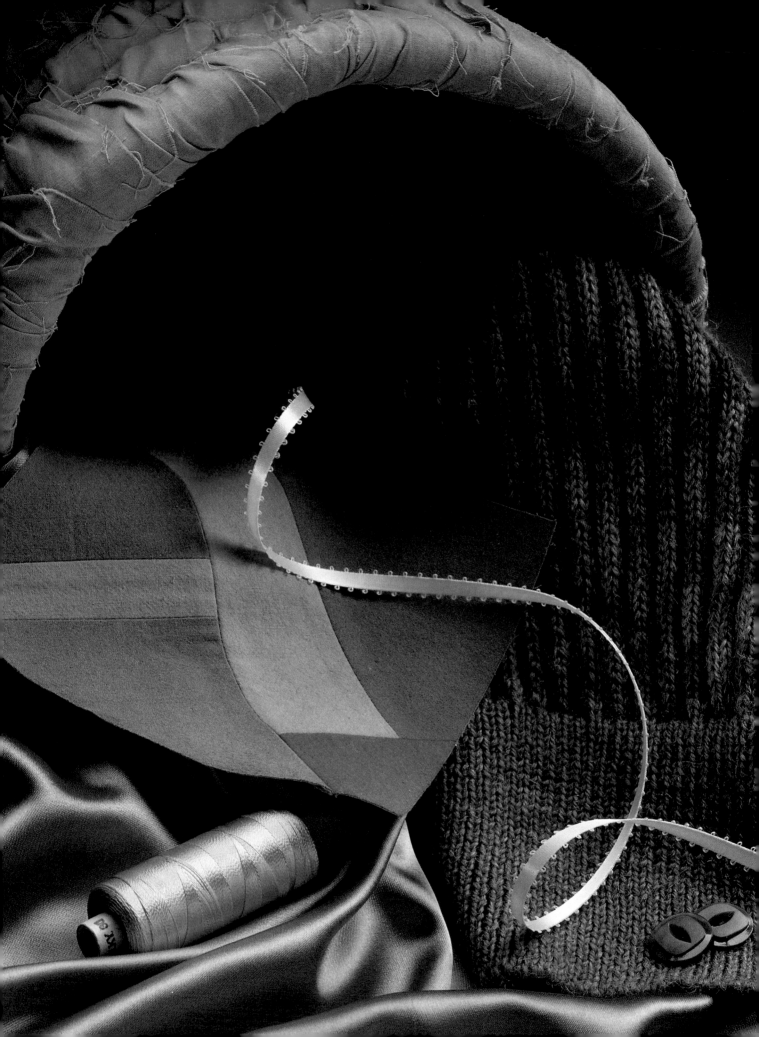

Introduction

As a home sewer, you are creating a unique project every time you sew, by selecting fabric, patterns, and trim. Extending your creativity is a natural, because you already have an idea of the design, color, and style options that you have to choose from. Expand your sense of color by hand dyeing your own fabric for a pieced or appliquéd garment or quilt. Or marble your own fabric for an accessory such as a scarf or napkins for your table setting.

The Creative Details section shows you how to look for and copy design details for that "designer" look. It also gives you some special couture techniques to make your tailored garments especially professional, with an added design touch, such as channel-stitched cuffs or bias-cut sleeves. Making battenberg lace for a garment or adding ruching gives a garment that unique touch.

Create your own fabrics by hand dyeing solids, or tie-dyeing or marbling your fabrics. Or create your own fabrics by combining and adding to laces, making heirloom fabric, or by using a combination of special needles and feet on your machine to create special effects. Add embellishments such as appliqués, beads, snaps, and trim to fabric or to a completed garment. Try a bit of piecing or a few prairie points, and incorporate them into a tie, vest, belt, or jacket. Or make a slashed, or "blooming," fabric inset.

The next section, Fiber Art, shows you how to work with fibers and make a variety of projects, such as rag baskets, braided rugs, or Christmas ornaments. These projects are unique and fun to do. Learn English smocking and make a Christmas ornament that is easy and uses only two smocking stitches. Baskets can be made by machine or by hand for two different looks. Learn color and design concepts for quilting and even hand-appliqué techniques.

The Creative Projects section gives you projects and ideas that utilize your new or heightened skills. Try your hand at some basic accessories that complete a special outfit, and be creative in the styling and interpretation. You can change projects such as the scarf by tie-dyeing your own silk, or add prairie points to the purse design. The final project ideas are ones for your home, such as a bed skirt with clustered gathers and coordinating pillow sham, a comforter cover from sheets, or a folding chair cover.

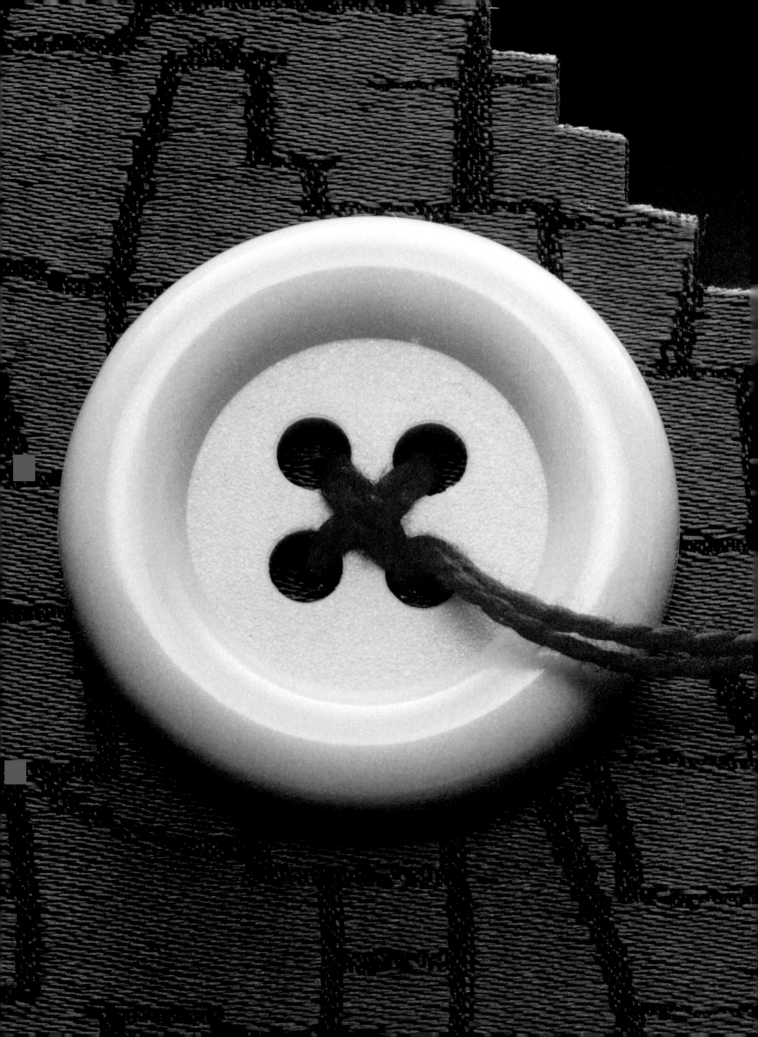

Creative Details

Discovering Design Details

Feel free to incorporate design details from other patterns, fashion magazines, ready-to-wear, or your imagination.

Some design details can be added without making a pattern; they need not be complicated to attract attention, and may simplify the construction of a garment and save time. One of the easiest is to eliminate facings whenever possible by substituting contrasting trim. This accomplishes two things: it eliminates bulk, and it provides design interest.

Try trimming wool with suede or leather, summerweight wovens like silk tweed or noile with linen, or cotton knits and wool jersey with a contrasting knit or ribbing. To ensure a smooth fit around curves, cut woven trim on the bias and cut knit trim on the crosswise grain. Suede and leather trim should be cut in the direction of greatest stretch. Synthetic suedes such as Ultrasuede® lack grain and may therefore be cut in any direction, since little stretch can be expected. Experiment on scrap fabric to get the desired effect.

Another simple design idea copied from ready-to-wear is the substitution of one large button for a series of buttons on a jacket (left). Choose the button carefully and it will become an accessory. Because a large buttonhole is seldom attractive, substitute a fabric loop sewn into the seam for the buttonhole closing.

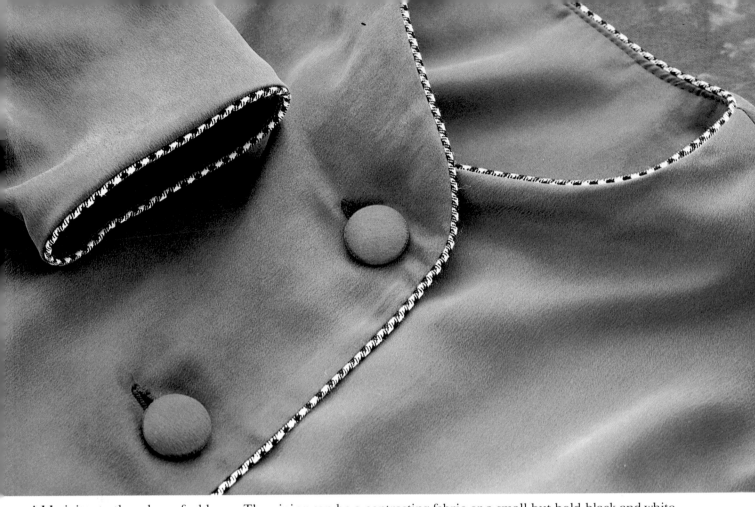

Add piping to the edges of a blouse. The piping can be a contrasting fabric or a small but bold black-and-white print. The facings need to be cut separately.

Trim a wool jacket by substituting suede or leather for a section of the garment, such as the front band, pocket flap, or cuff.

Roll-up sleeves on a jacket can become a fashion accent by facing the sleeves in a contrasting or coordinating fabric.

Copying Design Details

Garments and accessories with creative and interesting styling details command high prices, which cover not only originality, but construction time as well. This is where the home sewer has an advantage. High-fashion details rarely require additional fabric; it is simply a matter of investing a little extra time and knowing how to copy and add the detail. The end result is a unique garment with an expensive look.

Design details may be found anywhere from the "designer section" of the best department store to the trendiest boutiques in town. Or, turn to fashion magazines for inspiration. When shopping, keep an eye out for anything that seems well made or unique. Look closely at pockets, collars, lapels, topstitching, plackets, waistbands, and hem finishes. To a salesclerk, you are admiring the workmanship. As a sewer, you are subconsciously measuring and planning the steps to incorporate this detail into your next garment.

Since rulers and measuring tapes do not create goodwill in a ready-to-wear store, body parts must act as your measuring devices. Pocket width may be the distance of five outstretched fingers. Flap detailing may be the depth of one thumb. Back hem length may be longer than the front by one forefinger. Note carefully the placement of the design detail on the garment itself. How far is the detail above or below the armhole? Is it centered or closer to the side or

front? How large are buttons — the size of a thumbnail or of the nail on your little finger?

Success in duplicating a design depends upon detailed observation. Record your observations the minute you leave the store. Do not rely on your memory. Always carry a notebook and pen in your purse to write down ideas for your next sewing project. Sometimes a design seen two years ago may be the perfect solution for customizing and creating additional interest for a current sewing project.

Another place to look for design detail inspiration might be right in your own closet. Look for a garment with a favorite pocket, waistband, yoke, cuff, or collar. Making a pattern of a design detail (opposite) is a simple process. The fastest way to make a pattern of the detail is to trace it with wax paper and a tracing wheel. This gives you a pattern minus the seam allowances.

Normally, when copying a finished garment, 5⁄8" (1.5 cm) seam allowances are added. Sometimes, adding and sewing a seam of 5⁄8" (1.5 cm) can result in a design detail that is slightly smaller than the original. For a more accurate copy, add up to 7⁄8" (2.2 cm) to cut edges, but stitch 5⁄8" (1.5 cm) seams. The amount to add to the cut edges will vary, depending on your tracing and cutting techniques, the size of the design detail, and the weight of the fabric. Now is the perfect time to change the design detail slightly, if desired.

How to Make a Pattern to Duplicate a Design Detail

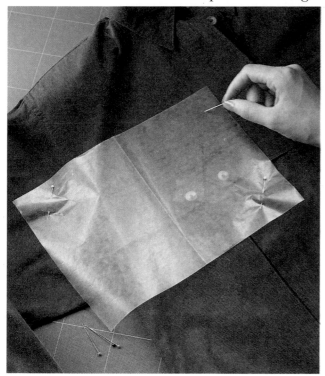

1) Fold or draw grainline on wax paper. Place paper over design detail, aligning grainlines. Pin to secure.

2) Trace around the finished edges of the design detail, using a tracing wheel.

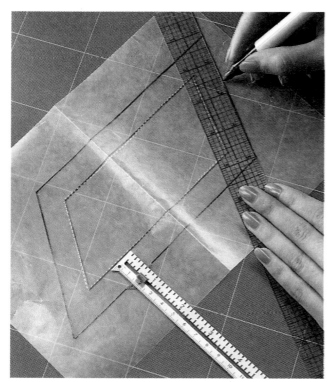

3) Remove paper from garment. If detail is symmetrical, fold along center line, and true edges. Add ⅝" to ⅞" (1.5 to 2.2 cm) to all cut edges. Depending on your tracing and cutting techniques, the size of the design detail, and the weight of the fabric, the amount to add to the cut edges will vary slightly.

4) Cut design detail according to pattern. Stitch, using a ⅝" (1.5 cm) seam allowance.

Couture
Sleeve Detail

Careful shaping and attention to detail in constructing sleeves makes them professional-looking. Once you have mastered the basics of sleeve construction, you may want to move beyond the instructions in your pattern envelope and add one or more of the following couture details to your sewing repertoire.

Shaped Center Seams

A popular design detail is the two-piece sleeve, with a center seam running from cap point to wrist. In this variation on a traditional tailored sleeve, all of the ease has been incorporated into the seam. The result is a sleeve that sets into a garment beautifully, requiring only a minimum of shaping.

In order to retain the shape of this type of sleeve, first sew the seam and press it open over a curved edge, such as a pressing ham or sleeve board, clipping where necessary. Then, apply interfacing. For a sleeve that will be lined, use a wool interfacing for a soft, cushioned seam; a stiff interfacing such as Sta-Form™ for a sharp, rigid seam; or hair canvas for a tailored seam, depending on the fabric of the garment. For an unlined sleeve, choose a bias strip cut from the fashion fabric or from silk organza.

Topstitching the center seam gives this two-piece construction more body and adds decorative detail. If topstitching is not used, the interfacing should be attached by hand to the seam allowances only.

Covered Shoulder Pads

Use covered shoulder pads in dresses, blouses, sweaters, and unlined jackets for a professional finish. Save money by covering pads with lining fabric or flesh-colored nylon tricot. A covered shoulder pad completes the look of couture sleeves.

How to Interface a Sleeve with Shaped Center Seam

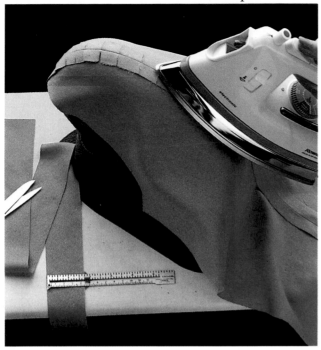

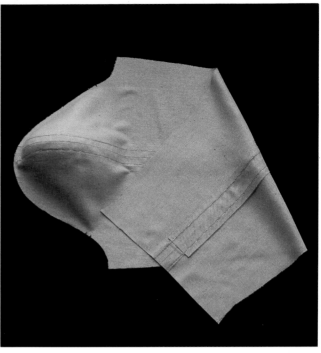

1) Cut interfacing on the bias 1¾" (4.5 cm) wide by finished length of sleeve. Stitch sleeve center seam. Press over a curved edge, clipping curves where necessary. Pin interfacing to sleeve, working from right side of sleeve.

2) Baste stitching lines through all thicknesses, with sleeve cap positioned on ham. Topstitch from hem edge on right side, ½" (3.8 cm) on each side of seam. If topstitching is eliminated, attach interfacing by hand to seam allowances only.

How to Cover Shoulder Pads

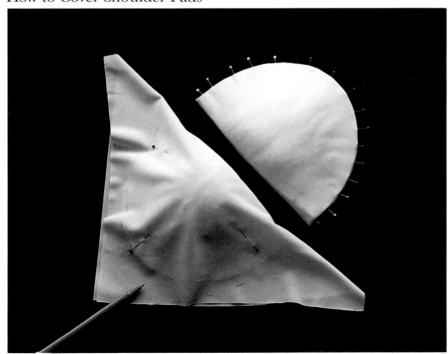

1) Cut a 12" (30.5 cm) square of fabric. Place shoulder pad on fabric with armhole edge along the diagonal. Fold fabric over pad. All-bias fabric shapes easily to pad. Draw outline of pad, add ⅝" (1.5 cm) seam allowance, and cut. Serge around edges. Or fold seam allowances in on underside of pad, and slipstitch around cut edges.

2) Slipstitch a dart in underside to hold in contoured shape. Tack pointed ends to armhole seam allowances and rounded portion to shoulder seam.

Bias-cut Sleeves

A beautiful effect can be achieved by cutting sleeves on the bias. Bias-cut sleeves also provide an easy solution to the problem of matching plaids from garment body to sleeve.

Cutting sleeves on the bias changes how a sleeve will drape and is especially effective with softer fabrics. With a solid-colored fabric there is a subtle change. When a stripe is used to create a chevron pattern, this detail becomes the focal point of the garment.

Due to the nature of the grain, bias sleeves will hang thinner and longer than the same sleeve cut on the straight grain. Therefore, as with any bias garment, let sleeves hang after setting them into the garment for at least 24 hours before hemming or applying cuffs. Be sure to hang the garment with shoulder pads inserted, preferably on a padded hanger, so the sleeves will hang naturally.

Tips for Cutting and Sewing on the Bias

Cut seam allowances 1½" (3.8 cm) wide. When fabric is cut on the bias, an explosion of fibers occurs along the cut, making the edge significantly longer than the original and intended length. If you stitch too close to the edge, your stitching line will be too long, resulting in a buckled, puckered seam. Pressing cannot correct this problem. The solution is to stitch bias seams 1½" (3.8 cm) from the cut edges, where the fibers are still intact.

Mark stitching line to ensure stitching a straight seam when sewing on the bias.

Use the smallest needle size possible and a stitch length of 12 to 15 stitches per inch (2.5 cm).

Stretch seam slightly as you sew, to prevent stitches from breaking when you wear garment.

Trim the seam allowances after sewing seams, if required. It is not always necessary to trim bias seam allowances. On a skirt, for example, the extra fabric in the seam allowance provides additional support along the seamline.

Leave bias seam allowances unfinished; bias does not ravel.

How to Cut Sleeves on the Bias

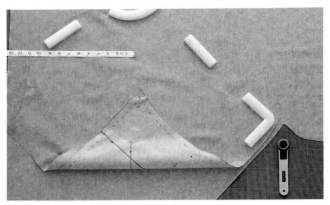

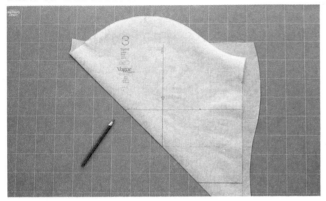

1) Fold pattern to form right angle at grainline marking. Mark new grainline along folded edge.

2) Place sleeve on single layer of fabric with new grainline on lengthwise grain of fabric; cap will point toward selvage. Cut, allowing 1½" (3.8 cm) seam allowances. Turn over pattern. Cut second sleeve with cap pointing toward opposite selvage.

How to Cut a Chevroned Bias Sleeve

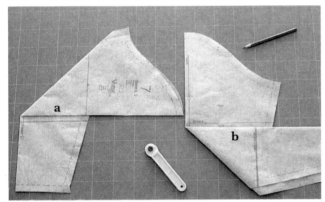

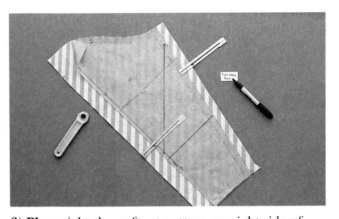

1) Fold pattern at center from shoulder dot to lower edge. For down-pointing chevron, fold pattern again from top to form right angle (**a**); diagonal crease is new grainline. Or, for up-pointing chevron, fold pattern from bottom to create new grainline (**b**). Cut pattern apart at center line.

2) Place right sleeve front pattern on right side of single layer of striped fabric, with new grainline following stripe; cut with 1½" (3.8 cm) lengthwise seam allowances. Mark lengthwise stitching lines on wrong side of fabric. Mark each sleeve section on wrong side as it is cut.

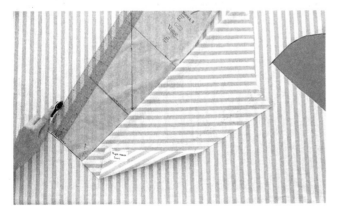

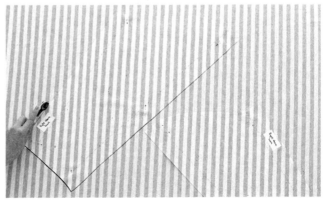

3) Place right sleeve front, right side up, on fabric; position next to right sleeve back pattern, matching stripes at a right angle to create a chevron at center *seamline*. Cut right sleeve back.

4) Cut the front and back for left sleeve using right sleeve pieces as a pattern. Place right sides of fabric together, matching stripes.

17

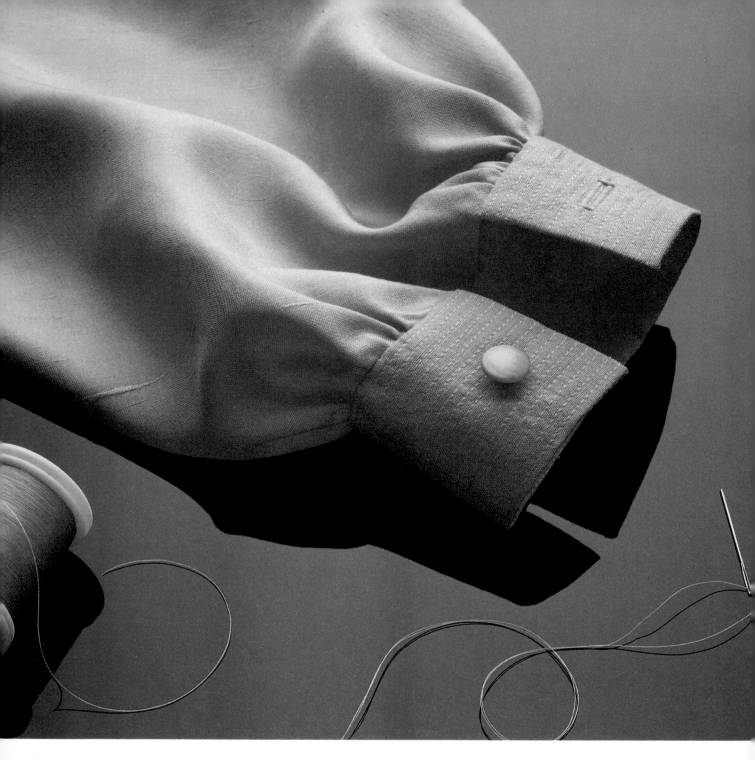

Channel-stitched Cuffs

Channel-stitching, a popular design detail, appears on cuffs, yokes, collars, and plackets. These closely spaced, parallel rows of stitches may look as if they were added to a completed garment as an afterthought, but for a couture look, they must be part of the construction process.

Shaping techniques, such as applying steam, heat, and pressure to add curve to flat fabric, are also crucial to achieving a couture finish for a garment. A cuff, for example, needs to wrap naturally around the wrist

for a polished look. Shaping techniques ensure that it will, by eliminating the excess facing and interfacing fabric that results when the three layers of a cuff are curved.

Couture sewing is an art. Practicing couture techniques requires a commitment to sharpen sewing skills beyond the basics. That commitment is amply rewarded in professional-looking garments and personal satisfaction.

How to Channel-stitch and Shape a Cuff

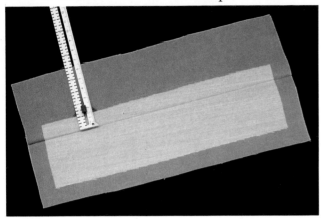

1) Cut interfacing for cuffs, extending ⅝" (1.5 cm) over center fold. Baste or fuse to the wrong side of fabric, on the side that will face outward on garment.

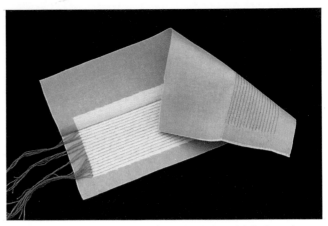

2) Stitch along fold line on right side of fabric using 15 to 20 stitches per inch (2.5 cm); begin and end at seamlines. Stitch parallel lines ⅛" (3 mm) apart; do not stitch in seam allowances. Tie off threads on wrong side.

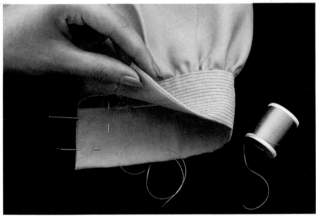

3) Stitch cuff to sleeve, right sides together. Press seam allowances toward cuff; grade. Fold cuff under at fold line, working from right side of cuff. Turn seam allowances under on long edge and ends, so cuff curves as it will when it is worn. Baste, using silk thread.

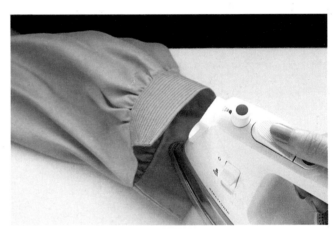

4) Steam inside cuff gently on ironing board, so it shrinks slightly.

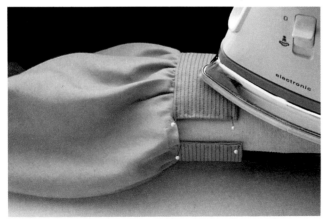

5) Wrap cuff around seam roll. Pin, and gently steam and press from right side. Repeat as necessary to shape cuff. Allow to dry completely.

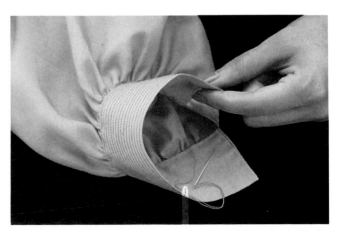

6) Slipstitch long edge and ends of cuff by hand. Cuff will retain shape without excess fabric on inside.

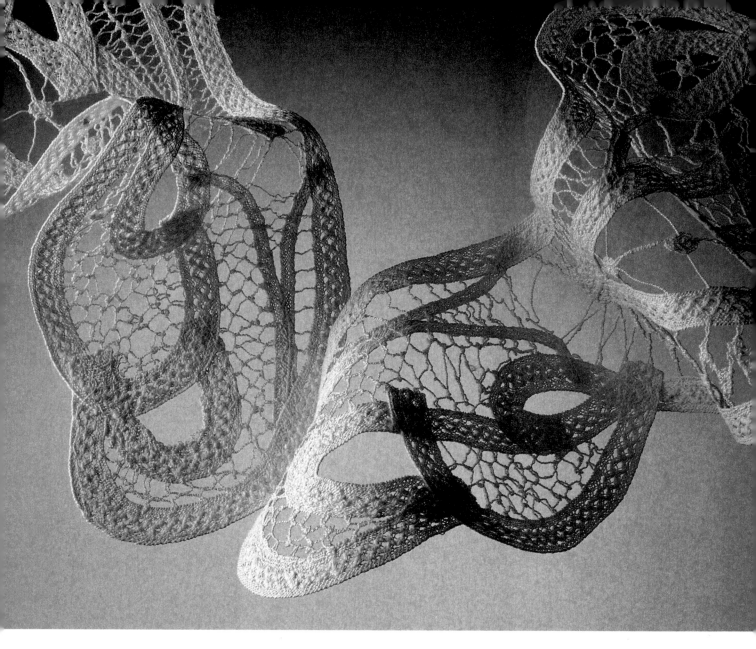

Creating Lace by Machine

A wide variety of patterns, kits, and specialty tapes are available for making battenberg lace either by hand or on the sewing machine. The procedure for making battenberg lace on the sewing machine is not difficult, but requires practice and a steady hand. It is done by a process of guiding the fabric by hand under the machine needle. In working patterns and fill-in stitches, the hand is the guide and skill is required to obtain a uniform and even stitch.

Use machine embroidery thread that matches the battenberg tape. Use the same thread in both the needle and the bobbin. A 50-weight or 60-weight cotton thread should be used to secure the tape, and a 30-weight cotton thread is used for the fill-in stitches. A size 70/9 or 80/11 needle is recommended for use. A 6" to 10" (15 to 25.5 cm) wooden embroidery hoop with a fixing screw, or a spring hoop, is necessary.

The base material to which the tape is glued and stitched is a water-soluble stabilizer. It is a translucent plasticlike material that completely dissolves in water. The battenberg tape is bias woven with a heavy edge thread. Selectively pulling this thread on the inner edge of a curve will cause the tape to contour in a flat and uniform manner to create your design.

Spending a little time perfecting your technique will be well worth while. Experiment by working in an area outside the work, adjusting tension for a balanced stitch. Run the machine at a steady speed, moving the work smoothly and continuously. When you need to stop, stop at a point on the tape. To avoid a lot of starting and stopping, make long stitches along the edge of the tape to the next fill-in stitch. Plan your stitch pattern ahead to avoid erratic motions and irregular stitches. If the stabilizer tears when working, use a double layer.

How to Make Battenberg Lace on the Sewing Machine

1) **Trace** pattern onto stabilizer, using a water-soluble pen. Form tape to traced pattern, pinning in place; contour tape as necessary by pulling heavy edge thread on tape. Secure shaped design to stabilizer, using glue stick.

2) **Place** a section of stabilizer in 6" (15 cm) embroidery hoop, exposing a section of pattern. Remove presser foot; cover or lower the feed dogs. Set stitch control for straight stitch; lower the presser foot bar. Stitch around outer edges of tape; where edges abut, secure edges together using a zigzag motion.

3) **Cut away** stabilizer in design area. Work fill-in stitches in open areas by stitching from one tape edge to the other and securing thread at edges of tape with three or four short stitches; zigzag over base threads to complete each section of design.

How to Apply Lace

4) **Cut away** stabilizer near outer edge of work. Rinse finished piece in warm water, dissolving any remaining stabilizer.

5) **Lay** the wet piece of battenberg lace between layers of bath towel, and pat dry. Place lace face down on padded surface; block by hand, using pattern as guide. Press with iron on cotton setting to shrink tape and threads; starch, if desired.

Pin finished lace to fabric in desired position. Uncover the feed dogs or raise them. Attach presser foot. Stitch lace to garment on outer edge of tape, using narrow zigzag stitch. Cut away fabric under the lace carefully, using embroidery scissors.

Ruching

Ruches may be either applied to the fabric surface or inset; they will add surface relief and bulk. Entire sections of a garment can also be ruched. Choose fabrics that enhance the technique itself. They should reflect light, because the play of light on the folded or gathered surfaces is part of the effect. Fabrics like taffeta, satin, metallics, or iridescents are dramatic. Transparent fabrics like organza, chiffons, or voiles used in certain areas of a gown can create an interesting detail. Your imagination is the only limit to applying this technique to your projects.

Applied Ruches

For applied ruches, strips of ruched fabric or ribbon are attached to the surface of a garment. Most often with this technique, the ruched strip is applied by stitching down the middle. This allows the sides to lift up, giving an opportunity to finish the edges in a variety of ways.

Edge finishes may include decorative stitching by machine or by hand; "feathering," raveling the edges for a fringe; or a rolled hem stitched with a serger.

Applied ruched strips (left) can add fullness to a hemline, emphasize a sleeve, or even cover an entire evening gown for a stunning effect. Snail-shirred ruches (top three) add a soft, scalloped effect to a garment. Box-pleated ruches (bottom two) can be embellished by joining pleats together with beading or embroidery.

Ruched garment section (page 25) adds texture and surface interest to a princess-style knit dress.

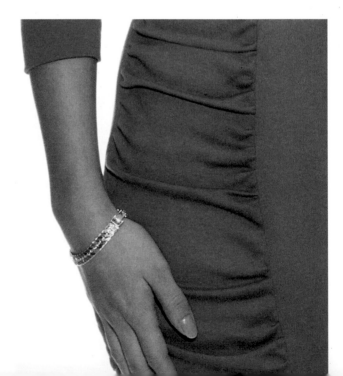

Tips for Sewing Ruches

Sew a test sample to determine the amount of fullness suitable for your fabric. Experiment to achieve the look you want.

Cut ruches on the bias if raveling or shaping around curves is a problem. Cutting on the bias also lessens the need for pressing.

Add a flat piece of fabric as a stabilizer to the wrong side of a ruched strip if the shape of the garment might shift.

Gathered inset ruche (page 26) accents the design line of a jacket.

Box-pleated applied ruche (page 24) adds flair to the sleeve edge on an evening dress. Snail-shirred applied ruches are a softer alternative.

Triangle-tipped inset ruche (page 27) adds a sophisticated note to evening pants.

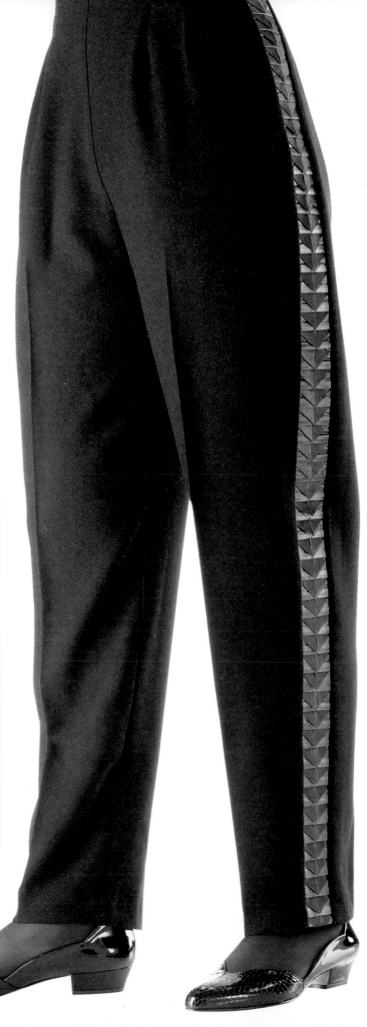

How to Make a Snail-shirred Applied Ruche

1) Cut fabric strip on lengthwise grain to desired width and two to three times finished length. Finish edges as desired. Fold strip on true bias lines; press folds.

2) Stitch a continuous gathering line, following bias folds. Draw threads to gather. Apply to the garment, sewing by hand or by machine along gathering stitches.

How to Make a Box-pleated Applied Ruche

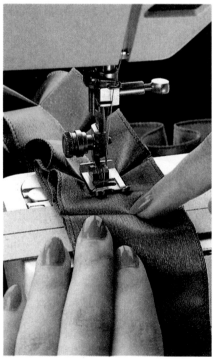

1) Cut fabric strip on straight grain to the desired width and three times the finished length. Cut cardboard template the desired depth of each pleat and two times as wide as strip. Mark center line of template.

2) Finish edges of fabric strip as desired. Fold strip over template, forming pleat; finger-press. Remove template and stitch along center of strip to secure pleat. Repeat to end of fabric strip.

3) Pinch opposite sides of each box pleat together. Tack at center of upper edge by hand or by machine. Stitch a bead at the center of each pleat when tacking, if desired.

Ruched Garment Sections

A commercial pattern may be adapted to create a garment with a ruched section, such as the dress pictured on page 22. Use this method for ruching an entire garment section, or just a portion of it. Depending on the pattern and the fabric, it may be necessary to stabilize the ruched area with a backing fabric, so the garment retains its shape when worn. A soft, lightweight fabric, such as chiffon or tricot, may be used for the stabilizer. For more body in the ruched area, use a firmer, crisp stabilizer, such as taffeta or organdy.

How to Ruche a Garment Section

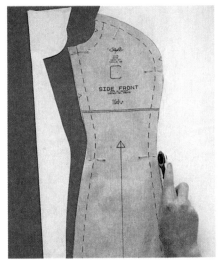

1) **Cut** fabric for stabilizer, if desired, from the section of pattern piece to be ruched.

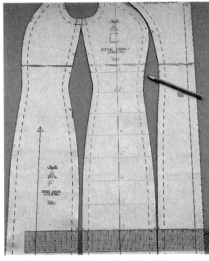

2) **Mark** where ruche begins and ends on the pattern piece to be ruched, and on adjacent pieces. Extend grainline to length of pattern piece. Draw parallel lines 2" to 3" (5 to 7.5 cm) apart in area to be ruched. Number sections.

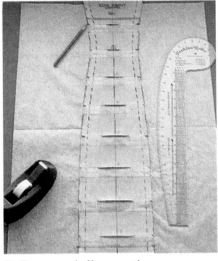

3) **Draw** grainline on tissue paper; lay pattern on top. Cut pattern on marked lines. Expand ruched section one and one-half to three times in length, distributing extra length evenly. Draw cutting lines and seamlines. Mark ends of ruched area.

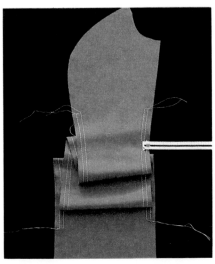

4) **Cut** out garment; transfer the pattern markings. Stitch two rows of gathering stitches ¼" (6 mm) apart on edges to be ruched, with first row just inside seamline.

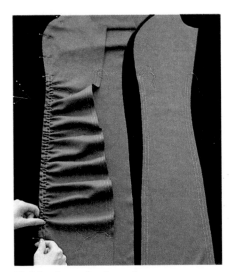

5) **Match** ruched section to garment section, pulling up gathers evenly and aligning markings; pin. Baste stabilizer, if used, to wrong side of ruched section. Stitch seams with ruched section up.

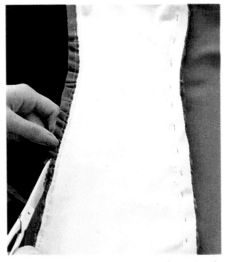

6) **Trim** seam allowances of ruched section. Finish seam allowances separately. Press seam allowances toward flat section.

Inset Ruches

Ruches may be inserted into a seamline to accent a design line on the pattern. Or, add your own design line to a garment by cutting a garment section apart and inserting a ruche.

Inset ruches may either be gathered or pleated. Gathered inset ruches may be gathered equally on both sides and inserted in a straight seamline, or unequally, to follow a curved seamline. Pleated inset ruches, such as triangle-tipped ruches, are inserted only in straight seams. Stabilize inset ruches with a lightweight backing fabric applied to the wrong side of the ruche, if necessary.

How to Adjust a Pattern for an Inset Ruche

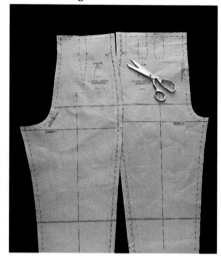

Add ruche centered on seamline.
Draw new cutting lines (red) one-half the finished width of ruche from edge on both pattern pieces. Draw the new seamlines (blue); transfer the pattern markings.

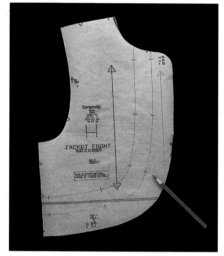

Add ruche to garment section.
1) Mark desired finished width of ruche on pattern. Add markings for alignment. Draw a grainline on outer piece.

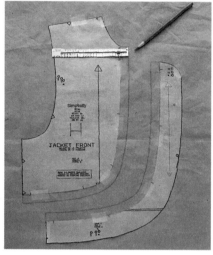

2) **Cut** pattern apart on marked design lines; add ⅝" (1.5 cm) seam allowances.

How to Sew a Gathered Inset Ruche

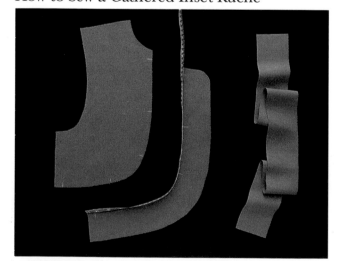

1) **Adjust** pattern, above. Cut out garment. Measure seamline where ruche will be inserted; on curved seamlines, measure longest edge. Cut fabric strip for ruche one and one-half to three times the length of seamline by the desired finished width plus 1¼" (3.2 cm) for seam allowances.

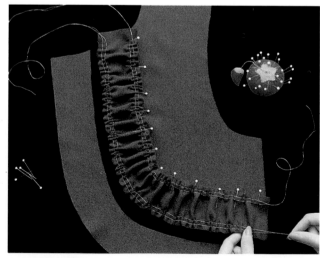

2) **Gather** edges of ruche, and pin, right sides together, to fit garment edges. On curved ruches, gathers will be tighter on inside curve. Stitch to garment, gathered side up. Grade seam allowance of ruched strip before finishing edges. Press the seam allowances toward the unruched sections.

How to Sew a Triangle-tipped Inset Ruche

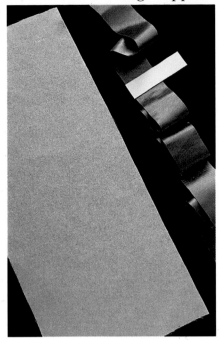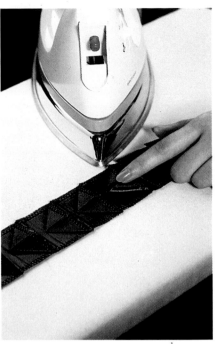

1) Adjust pattern, opposite. Cut out garment. Cut fabric strip for ruche five to six times the finished length by desired width plus ½" (1.3 cm) for seam allowances. Cut cardboard template one-half the width of strip plus ⅛" (3 mm) by two times the width of strip.

2) Finish edges of fabric strip by serging or zigzag stitching. Fold fabric strip over the cardboard template and press into pleats; space pleats ¼" (6 mm) apart.

3) Fold each pleat again so corners meet in center; press. Continue to fold and press, forming a series of triangles.

4) Fold fabric between triangles to form narrow pleat, so each triangle slightly overlaps the preceding one, covering raw edges. Press edges sharply. Tack invisibly along center back, catching underlayer only.

5) Finish seam allowances of garment. Pin ruche to garment, right sides together; match seamlines and align markings across ruche. [Ruche has ¼" (6 mm) seam allowances.] Stitch, ruche side up. Press seam allowances toward unruched sections.

Creating Your Own Fabric

Creating Hand-dyed Fabric

The range of colors possible in hand-dyed fabrics is greater than that available commercially. Hand-dyed fabric gives you a sequence of colors, ranging from light to dark, or makes a smooth transition from one color to another. It also allows you to create a specific color that may not currently be in style.

Using just five colors of dye, the primaries (red, yellow, and blue) plus black and brown, you can dye literally thousands of colors. You can create fabric colors that are intense or subdued, pale or dark. You can dye fabrics in a rainbow of colors and a wide range of neutrals. The possibilities are endless.

For hand dyeing, a Procion® fiber-reactive dye is recommended. These are the dyes the textile and garment industries use. Procion dyes bond with fabric, and are lightfast and washfast. Procion dyes produce a transparent color. This means the dye penetrates the fabric rather than sitting on top. This also means the weave structure of the fabric is visible and there is no change in the feel of the fabric.

Procion dyes can be used on all natural fibers, from cotton to silk to rayon. They do not work on synthetic fabrics or blends containing synthetics. They work in a warm-water dye bath, so no heating or boiling is required, just warm tap water. And, compared to other dyes, fiber-reactive dyes are relatively safe to use.

Although these dyes are some of the safest available for hand dyeing, remember that dyes are chemicals and that dyeing is chemistry. Avoid any direct skin contact with the dyes and the setting chemicals by wearing long pants and a long-sleeved shirt, and by protecting your hands with rubber gloves. Avoid inhaling the dye powders; always use a face mask. A pollen mask is adequate unless you do a lot of dyeing, in which case, a professional respirator is recommended. Liquid Procion dyes are available, but they are somewhat less stable and less colorfast than powdered Procion dyes. However, they do not pose the hazard of breathing airborne dye particles.

Never eat, drink, or smoke while dyeing, so you do not ingest any dye powder or solution. Do not dye in your kitchen or any other eating area. Do not dye if you are pregnant. Keep dyes, as you would any chemicals, out of the reach of children. And use your dyeing equipment only for dyeing. Never use your measuring spoons and cups for cooking, too! If you follow these instructions and use common sense, dyeing can be safe.

The equipment needed for dyeing includes buckets, spoons, cups, rubber gloves, and a face mask, and can be found at your local grocery, hardware, or drugstore.

Two of the chemicals needed for dyeing are available from your grocery store: salt (either iodized or non-iodized) and water softener. Dyes, washing soda (also known as soda ash), and Synthrapol® (a special detergent) are available from weavers' supply stores or by mail order. Do not be tempted to buy washing soda from the grocery store because it contains bleach.

The easiest technique to use with fiber-reactive dyes is immersion dyeing: the fabric is put into the dye pot and comes out one color. You can modify the technique by blocking part of the fabric from dye penetration by folding and tying it.

Guidelines for Dyeing

Two basic aspects to consider when mixing colors are hue and value. Tints are lighter values; shades are darker values. It is possible to dye any color, but the way you achieve each depends on whether it is a hue, a tint, or a shade. Test the hue on a fabric scrap when mixing the dye concentrate.

Hues are created by mixing the primary colors red, blue, and yellow in various proportions. The concept is simple: red plus yellow makes orange; red plus blue makes violet; and blue plus yellow makes green. Vary the proportions, and you get greenish blues, reddish oranges, and so on.

For most colors, a total of six teaspoons (30 mL) of dye powder per yard (0.95 m) of fabric gives a strong hue. Because the primary colors have different strengths, the proportion of each color you need to mix to get a specific hue will vary. Yellow, for example, tends to be weaker than blue, so mixing three teaspoons (15 mL) of each will not give a true green; rather, more of a blue-green. The chart at left shows the proportions for mixing secondary colors, such as violet, and tertiary colors, such as red-violet and blue-violet. To create other hues, experiment to find the proper amounts to mix, always maintaining the six-teaspoon (30 mL) total per yard (0.95 m) of fabric.

When mixing two hues to produce a third hue, you can generally tell what the third hue will be by dipping a scrap of fabric into the concentrated dye mixture, as in step 2, page 34.

	Red	Red-Violet	Violet	Blue-Violet	Blue
Red Dye	6 tsp. (30 mL)	4½ tsp. (22.5 mL)	3 tsp. (15 mL)	1½ tsp. (7.5 mL)	0
Blue Dye	0	1½ tsp. (7.5 mL)	3 tsp. (15 mL)	4½ tsp. (22.5 mL)	6 tsp. (30 mL)
	Blue	**Blue-Green**	**Green**	**Yellow-Green**	**Yellow**
Blue Dye	6 tsp. (30 mL)	3 tsp. (15 mL)	1 tsp. (5 mL)	¼ tsp. (1.25 mL)	0
Yellow Dye	0	3 tsp. (15 mL)	5 tsp. (25 mL)	5¾ tsp. (28.75 mL)	6 tsp. (30 mL)
	Yellow	**Yellow-Orange**	**Orange**	**Red-Orange**	**Red**
Yellow Dye	6 tsp. (30 mL)	5¾ tsp. (28.75 mL)	5 tsp. (25 mL)	3 tsp. (15 mL)	0
Red Dye	0	¼ tsp. (1.25 mL)	1 tsp. (5 mL)	3 tsp. (15 mL)	6 tsp. (30 mL)

Tints are achieved by decreasing the amount of dye powder in a dye bath. For a medium tint, use three teaspoons (15 mL) of dye powder per yard (0.95 m) of fabric; for a light tint, try one teaspoon (5 mL) per yard (0.95 m). With few exceptions, the value of dyed fabric is determined by how much dye powder is used, not by how long the fabric sits in the dye bath. Removing fabric from the dye bath early will only result in a fabric that is less lightfast and washfast. To dye a series of tints, use half the amount of dye for each piece of fabric. For example, to make four fabrics from true blue to light blue, mix four dye baths: the first using 6 teaspoons (30 mL) of dye, the second using 3 teaspoons (15 mL) of dye, the third using 1½ teaspoons (7.5 mL), and the fourth using ¾ teaspoon (3.75 mL).

Gray shades are achieved by adding black dye to a hue.

Shades are dyed by adding black or brown to a hue. Blacks and browns are very strong colors; it does not take much of them to darken a hue. Use a total of 6 teaspoons (30 mL) of dye powder per yard (0.95 m) of fabric; for example, ¼ teaspoon (1.25 mL) of brown plus 5¾ teaspoons (28.75 mL) of yellow. Experiment with proportions to achieve a particular shade.

Earth shades are achieved by adding brown dye to a hue.

Fabrics for Dyeing

Fabrics should be of all-natural fibers with no surface finish. Refer to the end of the fabric bolt to see if a fabric has been treated, for example, with a permanent-press finish. It is possible to dye a fabric with a permanent-press finish; however, it will take two to three times the amount of dye to produce a particular color, and it may be more difficult to dye it evenly.

Night-before Preparation

Wash fabric in Synthrapol® to remove sizing and to preshrink.

YOU WILL NEED

1 yd. (0.95 m) 100 percent cotton fabric, with no surface finish.

Synthrapol®, a special detergent (available from weavers' supply stores, and by mail order).

Procion® fiber-reactive dyes in red, blue, yellow, black, and brown for entire spectrum of possible colors (available from weavers' supply stores, and by mail order).

¼ **cup (59 mL) washing soda,** also called soda ash (available from weavers' supply stores, and by mail order). Do not use grocery store variety.

Plastic or enamel bucket, 3-gallon (11.4 L) capacity or larger.

Set of measuring spoons, set of measuring cups, plastic or wooden mixing spoons.

Rubber gloves.

Face mask (available from hardware, drug, or dime store).

1 cup (237 mL) salt, either iodized or non-iodized.

1 to 2 tablespoons (15 to 30 mL) water softener, if you have hard water.

Rubber bands or nylon cord, if tie-dying.

How to Dye One Yard of Cotton Fabric (immersion method)

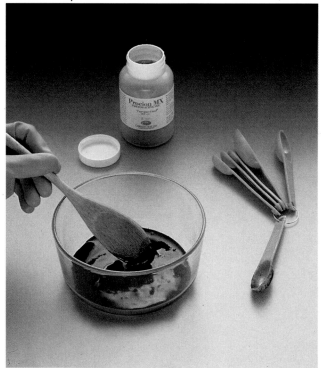

1) Mix dye powder with a little hot tap water to make a smooth paste (see chart, page 32, for quantity of powder). Add 1 cup (237 mL) warm water gradually, stirring until dye is dissolved.

2) Test hue by dipping the wet fabric scrap into dye concentrate. Test will be somewhat darker than final color, because fabric is still wet and dye concentrate is darker than the final dye bath. Adjust the hue, if necessary, by adding a little more of one of original dye colors (see pages 32 to 33).

3) Fill dye pot with 2 gallons (7.6 L) hot tap water. Add 1 cup (237 mL) salt and stir until dissolved. Stir in 1 to 2 tablespoons (15 to 30 mL) water softener for hard water. Stir in dissolved dye.

4) Add clean, thoroughly wet fabric to dye bath. Wearing rubber gloves, stir with your hands for 30 minutes; keep fabric submerged. Do not allow fabric to bunch up or to float above surface.

5) Dissolve 1/4 cup (59 mL) washing soda in 1 to 2 cups (237 to 473 mL) hot water and add to dye bath. Do not pour washing soda solution directly onto fabric. Stir briefly, making sure all the fabric stays submerged. Dye fabric 1 hour longer, stirring every 10 minutes.

6) Wash fabric in hot water, using Synthrapol. Dry in clothes dryer at hottest temperature for 30 minutes. Press.

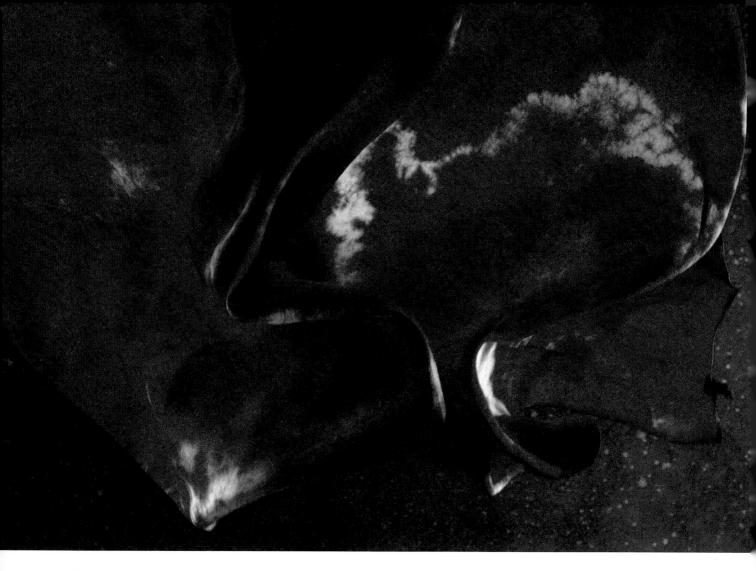

Tie-dyeing

Tie-dyeing involves folding, twisting, or scrunching fabric, then tightly tying off sections so the dye does not color the entire fabric. The tying, a resist technique, blocks part of the fabric from contact with the dye. Tie-dying is the easiest and most familiar resist technique. Rubber bands, cords, and strings are used to hold the fabric in place and block the dye from penetrating the fabric. Dye may be applied by the immersion method or direct application method.

Fabric or garments such as T-shirts, leggings, or items made of 100 percent cotton or silk may be tie-dyed. Other natural fibers including linen or rayon may be used. For silk, use cotton cord for tying. Innumerable combinations of color and patterns are possible, depending on how the fabric is folded and tied, and whether one or more colors are used. With some dyes, the various component colors penetrate fabric at different rates, resulting in a multicolored halo effect called starburst (opposite).

Folding the fabric in preparation for tying works best if the fabric is damp. Experiment with the tying techniques, using small pieces of fabric. For stripes and checks, use a 1/4-yard (0.25 m) square of fabric. For a starburst effect, use a 1/2-yard (0.50 m) fabric rectangle. Once you have mastered these methods of folding and tying, invent and experiment with other methods. You may want to sew your swatches together to make a unique quilt, or incorporate them into a garment as a decorative panel, a yoke, or a pocket facing.

By applying these tying techniques and color-mixing principles, you can dye fabric in any pattern, color, or range of colors imaginable. Practice using the three primary colors: red, blue, and yellow. Experiment by adding black and brown to create shades. Mix dyes to create a beautiful new color, then develop sequences of tints and shades using that color as your starting point. Or, create two new colors, and dye fabric to make a smooth transition between them. Then introduce pattern.

Immersion Method

After folding and tying, immerse the fabric bundle in a dye bath. See page 34 for a list of supplies and directions for preparing the fabric and the dye. Read the entire section on dyeing (pages 30 to 35), and follow any precautions given. Tie-dyed fabric may be immersed in successive dye baths for a multicolored effect. Fabric may also be retied and immersed to create more patterning.

Direct Application Method

The direct application method uses the same folding and tying techniques as above, but offers more control as to the placement of the dye. It is also easier to utilize more colors. The dye is applied with an applicator such as a squeeze bottle. Use the color guidelines on pages 32 and 33. Follow any precautions given on page 30.

Mix dye solution as follows to make 4 oz. (119 mL) of solution. Add 2 teaspoons (10 mL) dye, 1 tablespoon (15 mL) of urea and ⅛ teaspoon (0.7 mL) of water softener, if necessary, to ½ cup (119 mL) warm water. Mix thoroughly so dye is completely dissolved. This mixture should be used within two days. Tie or bundle as on pages 37 to 39. Apply dye directly to bundled fabric or garment from squeeze bottle. Dye may be applied exactly where desired.

YOU WILL NEED

Fabric or garment.

Synthrapol®, a special detergent, available at weavers' supply stores.

Procion® fiber-reactive dyes, available at weavers' supply stores.

¼ **cup (59 mL) soda ash**, available at weavers' supply stores. (Do not use grocery store washing soda.)

Let fabric sit on newspaper for an hour to soak up excess water. Carefully wrap in plastic wrap and let sit for at least two nights to allow dye to set. Seal the plastic completely. Open and lay the fabric on "clean" newspaper to dry. Allow fabric to sit at least 24 hours before washing to ensure maximum color. Rinse the fabric under running lukewarm water. Transfer immediately to hot water with 1 teaspoon (5 mL) per gallon (3.78 L) of Synthrapol® soap or 2 to 3 tablespoons for a washer load. Wash for ten minutes and rinse. After rinse water runs clear, dry fabric in dryer.

Deep, intense color may require double or triple the amount of dye and more rinsing. Reds require a lot of rinsing.

Night-before Preparation

Wash fabric in Synthrapol to remove sizing.

Soak in bucket of soda ash solution: use one cup (237 mL) of soda ash per gallon (3.78 L) of water, and soak overnight. Do not crowd fabric.

Set of measuring spoons, cups, and wooden mixing spoons.

Rubber gloves; face mask.

Urea, available at weavers' supply stores.

1 to 2 tablespoons (15 to 30 mL) water softener, such as Mataphos®, if you have hard water.

Squeeze bottles.

How to Make a Starburst Pattern

Immersion method. Bunch damp fabric into tight ball. Wrap tightly with nylon cord (you should not be able to get your fingers underneath cord). Tie ends to secure. Dye as on pages 34 and 35. A halo effect occurs when blue dye penetrates fibers farther than red.

Direct application method. Prepare fabric (as above) and bunch into tight ball; wrap tightly with cord. Apply dye from squeeze bottle. Follow directions (above) to complete.

How to Make a Striped Pattern

Immersion method. Fold damp fabric into pleats about 1" (2.5 cm) wide. Wrap rubber bands around pleated fabric, spacing closely for narrow stripes, farther apart for wide stripes. Dye as on pages 34 and 35.

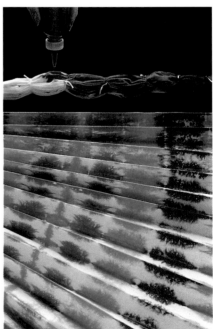

Direct application method. Prepare fabric (page 37). Fold into pleats and wrap as for immersion method (above). Prepare dye (page 37) and apply from squeeze bottle. Follow directions (page 37) to complete.

How to Make a Plaid Pattern

One-color plaid. Fold damp fabric into pleats about 2" (5 cm) wide. Fold pleated strip accordion-style, ending with a square bundle. Wrap nylon cord tightly around bundle, as if tying a package, wrapping several times in each direction. Dye as on pages 34 and 35.

Two-color plaid. Dampen dyed fabric. Refold into pleats; offset fold lines slightly from original ones, or as desired. Fold and wrap as in step 1. Dye with second color, as on pages 34 and 35.

Marbling Fabrics

Marbling is a way of decorating fabric or paper by floating pigments on a thickened water base, manipulating the pigments into a desired pattern, and transferring the pattern to fabric or paper. Probably the most familiar use of marbled paper was as endpapers in old books.

Marbling allows you to "paint" on fabric, even if you cannot draw. You do not need an extensive knowledge of color and design to produce beautiful results. It does not take a lot of space. It can be done using readily available, inexpensive materials. And the result of your efforts is unique.

Marbling is a printing process, and each print is one-of-a-kind. It can be done using paints, inks, dyes, or virtually anything that transfers color to fabric. It can work with almost any fabric, too, but usually the best results are achieved with natural fibers. Either white or colored fabrics can be used. However, the fabric color affects the results, since the coloring agents are very transparent. Texture is important, too; the smoother the surface of the fabric, the sharper the design.

To marble fabric, float drops of color on a thickened liquid base, stir them with a stick or comb to create the marbled pattern, and then lay the pretreated fabric on top to transfer the color. Rinse, dry, and heat-set, and the fabric is ready to be included in your next sewing project.

For simplicity, start with a small project, such as napkins. Use 100 percent cotton fabric and airbrush medium, a liquid paint packaged in squeeze bottles. Once you become proficient using these materials, you may want to experiment with larger pieces of fabric, other fibers, and different coloring agents. Acrylic tube paints and Turkish inks marble well, for example, and smooth silks accept the marbled color beautifully.

YOU WILL NEED

100 percent cotton fabric (must fit into pan without folding).

Ammonium alum (available from drugstores, art and craft supply stores, weavers' supply stores, and by mail order) to prepare fabric prior to marbling.

Basin or bucket for soaking fabric; rubber gloves.

Pan of nonporous material (such as a disposable aluminum pan) about 1½" to 3" (3.8 to 7.5 cm) deep and width and length larger than fabric to be marbled.

Small pan for testing how paints spread.

Carrageenan, a nontoxic emulsifier (available as a powder from art and craft supply stores, weavers' supply stores, and by mail order).

Blender for mixing carrageenan with water.

Airbrush medium in your choice of colors (available from art and craft supply stores, weavers' supply stores, and by mail order).

Orange stick or stylus and a hair pick for drawing through the paint.

Newspaper for cleaning base between prints.

Night-before Preparation

Fabric:

Wear rubber gloves when mixing ammonium alum.

Mix 4 to 6 tablespoons (60 to 90 mL) ammonium alum in 1 gallon (3.78 L) water in bucket.

Soak fabric in ammonium alum for 20 minutes, stirring once; wring fabric.

Dry mediumweight to heavyweight fabric in clothes dryer. Line dry fine cotton or silk; keep fabric wrinkle-free to avoid ammonium alum marks from uneven drying.

Press dry fabric with hot iron. Marble ammonium alum-treated fabric within one week. Wash out ammonium alum if fabric will not be marbled within one week.

Base:

Mix ½ to 1 level tablespoon (7.5 to 15 mL) powdered carrageenan in a blender full of warm water while agitating. Agitate 1 full minute.

Empty into pans. Mix more carregeenan as necessary to fill both large and small pans to depth of 1 inch (2.5 cm). Let stand overnight.

How to Marble Fabric

1) Drop paint on surface of carrageenan in small pan to test how well it floats. Drop carefully, taking care not to break surface of carrageenan. A drop should spread 1" to 3" (2.5 to 7.5 cm). If a color does not float well, add distilled water to paint, one drop at a time. If a color does not spread well, add rubbing alcohol to paint, one drop at a time. Test again.

2) Drop paints on carrageenan in large pan. Draw stylus slowly back and forth across surface, at about 1" (2.5 cm) intervals. Take care not to create bubbles by drawing too fast.

3) Draw stylus up and down across surface again at 1" (2.5 cm) intervals, perpendicular to first pattern.

4) Draw hair pick across surface. Hair pick may be drawn in any pattern you like, but usually perpendicular to direction of last drawing works best.

5) Lay ammonium alum-treated fabric on the base, lowering middle first, then easing ends down so no air gets caught between fabric and pigment. Pattern will adhere almost immediately to natural fiber fabrics. For blends, pat lightly to ensure printing.

6) Pull fabric over edge of pan, leaving as much base as possible. Rinse under running water to remove excess paint and base. If colors rinse out significantly, increase the proportion of ammonium alum when preparing fabric. The minerals in water affect this, so judge by trial and error. Wring fabric and line dry.

7) Clean base before marbling another piece of fabric, using newspaper folded to width of tray. Scrape paint off surface by pulling newspaper across base. Repeat marbling process for remaining fabric, beginning with step 2. Drop paints in same sequence to color-coordinate fabric. Age marbled fabric two weeks. Set color by drying in hot dryer 30 minutes.

Creative Lace

A large variety of laces (above) is available in fabric stores or by mail order. You can choose from many already-embellished laces, or add embellishments such as sequins, beads, soutache, and ribbon to plain lace. Color accents for lace include silvers and rainbow-hued iridescents as well as black accents on black lace for evening or white on white for the bride.

Lace fabric may be purchased and then embellished for a bodice or skirt of a garment. Or using appliqués

or insets on a wide range of garments is an easy way to add just a touch of lace. Lace appliqués and lace sections of a garment combine well with traditional fabrics, such as velvet, satin, and taffeta; or add lace to a tailored wool garment or a denim jacket to soften the look. Choose the type of lace according to the weight of the fabric with which it will be combined. For example, for a wool or denim jacket, use a heavier crocheted cotton lace.

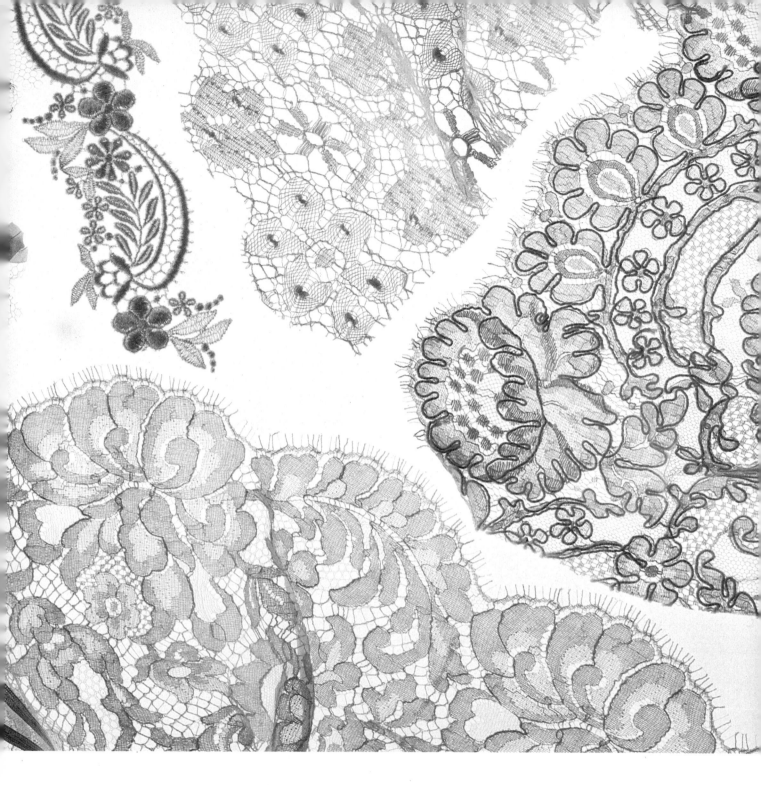

Tips for Sewing Lace

Use as few seams as possible. Choose a pattern with a simple design, and eliminate any unnecessary seams, such as straight center front or center back seams.

Wrap the toes of the presser foot with transparent tape, or cover the lace with tissue paper as you stitch, if the toes get caught in the lace while sewing. If the lace gets pulled down through the hole in the general-purpose or zigzag needle plate, put tissue paper under the fabric.

Study the lace design before you cut, to decide where to place seams and what technique to use to sew them. Because they are see-through, laces require seams that call as little attention to themselves as possible.

Mark pattern symbols that fall in an open space on the lace by placing a small piece of transparent tape on the wrong side of the fabric, and mark the symbol on the tape.

Creative Lace Ideas

In addition to sewing with lace, create your own lace fabric by adding embellishments to the lace, piecing it, or dyeing it.

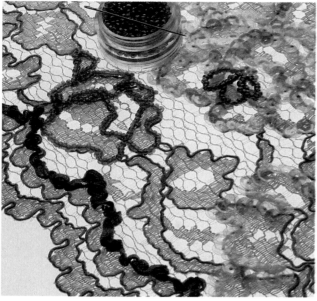

Add gathered ribbon, sequins, and strings of seed beads to lace fabric.

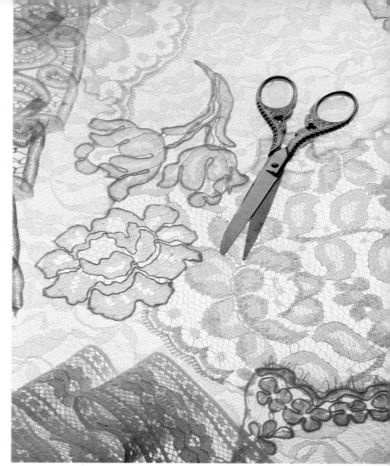

Make your own lace fabric from pieces of lace, either antique or new. Trim the underlap away. Individual motifs may be used to cover gaps between pieces. This process is similar to a crazy-quilt technique.

White lace can be dyed with tea or coffee to achieve an ecru or beige color. Test scraps of lace before dyeing entire piece. Rinse and let dry.

Creating
Heirloom Fabric

French hand sewing by machine creates intricate stitchery combined with delicate laces for exquisite projects in hours instead of days. Combine laces and French hand sewing to produce wedding gowns or christening dresses. Other possibilities include detachable collars, decorative yokes, and fancy pinafores.

There are several types of laces and trims made specifically for French hand sewing. Insertion lace has two straight finished sides. Beading lace has evenly spaced openings to allow for ribbon insertion. Edging laces are made with a shaped edge on one side and a straight edge on the other. Combinations of these laces may be made or purchased already joined together. Entredeux is a trim that is made with seam allowances to allow for easy application. Entredeux trim is available in several widths, and is usually white or cream.

Purchase laces and trims by mail or in specialty shops. Select lightweight fabrics such as batiste, organdy, and voile, in cotton or blends in white, ecru, or pastels; fine thread and needles work best. Starch and press all fabrics and trims except puffing strips.

Heirloom Trims

There are a variety of strips (above) that can be sewn together to form heirloom fabric. Sew the strips together with a narrow zigzag stitch. When strips are attached to entredeux, the needle needs to go into the holes in the entredeux. Make heirloom fabric larger than the section of garment that will be cut from it. As you sew, check periodically to make sure your needles are sharp and unblemished.

The following are seven types of strip that can be combined for heirloom fabric:

1) **Ribbon twists** add dimension to heirloom sewing projects, using ⅛" (3 mm) wide satin ribbon and decorative sewing machine stitches. Mark vertical lines on fabric and crossmarks at 2" to 3" (5 to 7.5 cm) intervals. At top crossmark, sew ribbon to fabric with a single decorative stitch pattern. Gently twist ribbon 180°, and secure again at next crossmark.

2) **Decorative openings** are created by winged needles, which have extensions on the sides. Stitch with machine embroidery thread and straight, zigzag, or decorative stitches. Sew on fabric that has been pressed extra crisp with several applications of spray starch.

3) **Pin tucks** are created with a pin-tuck foot and twin needles on any zigzag machine. Mark rows with a fabric marker. Attach pin-tuck foot, and stitch the first tuck. Grooves on the bottom of the foot channel fabric as you stitch the remaining tucks.

4) **Entredeux,** a connecting trim, bridges fabrics or laces. Place entredeux and fabric right sides together, raw edges even. With entredeux on top, stitch in the groove. Cut ¼" (6 mm) seam allowances, and finger-press them away from the trim. From the right side, zigzag to secure, with a zig in the fabric and a zag in the opening.

5) Puffing strips are made with fabric cut 1" to 2" (2.5 to 5 cm) wide and at least twice as long as the desired finished length. Gather both edges, by using two rows of straight stitching or by zigzagging over pearl cotton thread. Pin the strip to your ironing board, and adjust gathers. Steam, do not press, and let it dry. On a serger, stitch both sides without stopping. Place pearl cotton thread between the needle and the upper blade, leaving a tail behind your presser foot. Serge one side, continue with a chainstitch off the fabric, and serge the remaining side. Gather by pulling on both ends of the pearl cotton thread. Then pin, steam, and let dry.

6) Edging lace is an ideal finish for cuffs and hemlines. Place lace and fabric right sides together, extending fabric ⅛" (3 mm) beyond the straight edge of the lace. Stitch with a small zigzag, encasing extra fabric in your seam. When using a serger, prepare for a rolled hem with a short stitch length. Serge fabric and laces, right sides together. Open and press the seam flat.

7) Insertion lace can be alternated with ribbons or other laces; butt straight edges, and zigzag, placing a zig in one strip and a zag in the other. On a serger, flatlock laces, wrong sides together, guiding them ⅛" (3 mm) to the left of the blade. After stitching, pull the seam flat. For cutwork, place the lace on top of the fabric, and attach with a small zigzag. Turn the piece over, and carefully trim away the fabric.

Creating Special Effects

Creative expression and surface design can be enhanced by use of specialized presser feet and needles. Wing needles used with the special-purpose presser foot and twin needles used with the pin-tuck foot can create a handworked look in much less time.

A glance through any collection of fine table and bed linens reveals examples of the delicate craft of hemstitching. On antique linens, hemstitching was done by hand. Selected threads were drawn out of the fabric, and stitches were taken on the remaining threads to create a variety of lacelike effects. New versions are most often done by machine. Threads may still be drawn out of the fabric but, more often, they are simply pushed aside. The technique is easy to do on any zigzag sewing machine. All it takes is a single-wing or double-wing needle.

Wing needles, so named because they appear to have "wings" on their sides, push the threads aside, producing the characteristic "holes" of hemstitched

fabric. Double-wing needles feature a wing needle and a standard needle on one shank.

Hemstitching is most successful on delicate, crisp, natural fiber fabrics such as handkerchief linen, organdy, and organza. The fabric must be woven loosely enough so that the wing needle can push the yarns aside without damaging them. And it must have enough body so that the hole made by the needle does not close again immediately afterward.

Hemstitching on the bias or crosswise grain produces a more open look than on the lengthwise grain, so cut out pattern pieces accordingly. For example, if you wish to hemstitch down the center of a blouse, cut that piece on the bias or crosswise grain.

A basic zigzag stitch gives interesting effects when sewn with the single-wing needle. Sew directly on the project, or hemstitch strips or blocks to insert in or appliqué to the fabric.

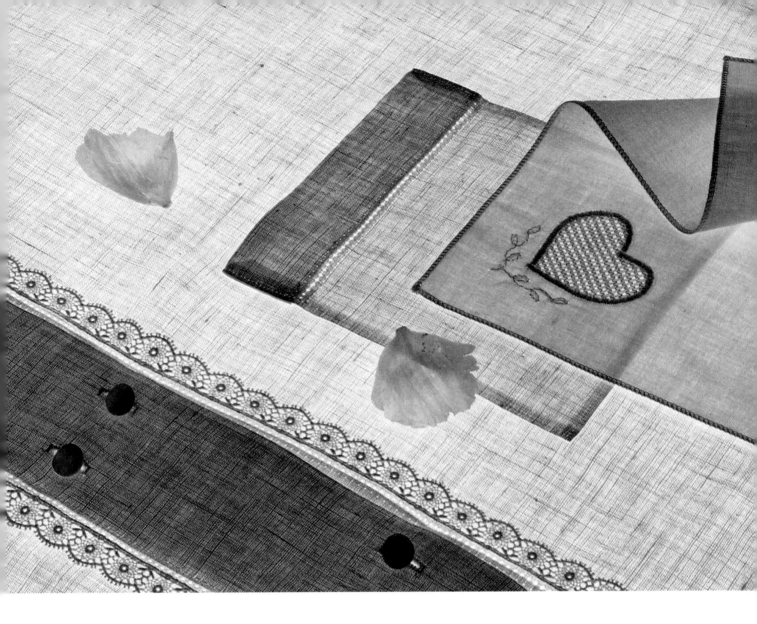

To achieve the look of entredeux, use a double-wing needle and a straight stitch. Sew twice, once up and then back, to get the effect. This is a nice technique for sewing hems or attaching lace.

Most machines come with a special-purpose presser foot, sometimes called a satin stitch foot, that has been designed specifically for satin stitching (a very close zigzag). This foot has a wide channel on the underside, behind the needle hole. This creates a "tunnel" through which emroidery and satin stitches can pass without piling up or being flattened.

Depending on the machine, special-purpose feet are available in metal or clear plastic. The clear plastic and open-toed-metal versions make it easier to follow a marked line, when monogramming, quilting, or appliquéing.

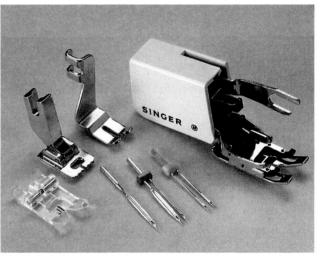

Feet, left to right: special-purpose foot, pin-tuck foot, gathering foot, Even Feed™ foot. Needles, left to right: single-wing needle, double-wing needle, twin needle.

How to Hemstitch Using a Double-wing Needle and Special-purpose Presser Foot

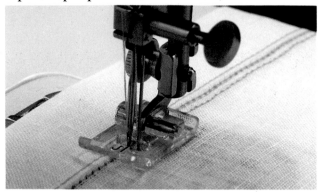

Stitching a hem. 1) Press double-fold hem in sheer fabric. Insert the double-wing needle and special-purpose presser foot. From right side, position fabric so standard needle stitches hem edge and wing needle pierces single layer of fabric. Stitch, using straight stitch.

2) Turn fabric at end of stitching. Stitch again; stitch slowly and make sure wing needle enters holes exactly on first line of stitching.

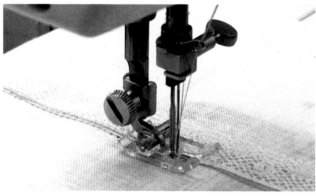

Attaching lace. 1) Insert double-wing needle and special-purpose presser foot. Mark stitching line with chalk. Position straight edge of lace along marked line. Stitch, using straight stitch with standard needle piercing edge of lace and wing needle piercing fabric only.

2) Turn fabric at end of stitching. Stitch again; stitch slowly and make sure wing needle enters holes exactly on first line of stitching.

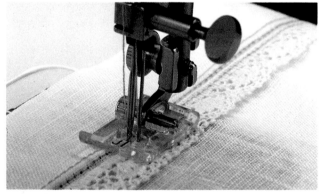

Stitching hem with lace. 1) Press double-fold hem in sheer fabric. Insert double-wing needle and special-purpose presser foot. From right side, position fabric so the standard needle stitches the hem edge and the wing needle pierces the single layer of fabric. Stitch, using straight stitch.

2) Turn fabric at end of stitching. Position lace edge next to first row of hemstitching. Stitch slowly, making sure wing needle enters holes exactly on first line of stitching and straight needle pierces edge of lace.

How to Hemstitch an Insert Using a Single-wing Needle and Special-purpose Presser Foot

1) Set machine for zigzag stitch of medium width and length. Stitch a section of organdy fabric slightly larger than motif to be appliquéd; begin first row of stitching on bias grain, using single-wing needle and special-purpose foot.

2) Turn at end of row, keeping tip of needle in fabric. Stitch next row so the needle pierces holes on one side of the previous row with every other swing. Continue stitching in this manner until block is covered.

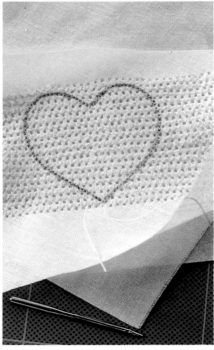

3) Place stabilizer under area of garment to be appliquéd. Straight-stitch appliqué to garment on outer edge of design, using embroidery hoop, if necessary, to keep fabric from puckering.

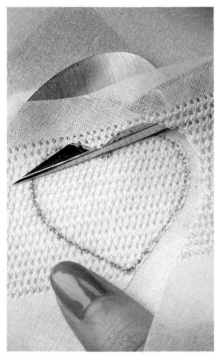

4) Cut excess appliqué fabric close to stitching line. Duckbill appliqué scissors help to cut close without cutting into stitches.

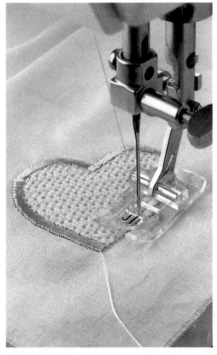

5) Stitch over previous stitching line and cut edge, using satin stitch. For extra emphasis, satin-stitch again, using a slightly wider stitch.

6) Remove stabilizer. Trim away fabric under hemstitched motif.

Pin-tuck design in synthetic suede makes an attractive pillow. Gathered pillow was done by using the gathering foot, which is helpful in many home decorating projects. Even Feed™ foot sews stripes without slippage.

Accessories for Special Effects

Pin tucks are one of the most versatile of all decorative effects. They look tailored when sewn vertically on a crisp shirt, demure across the yoke of a soft blouse, and ethnic when alternated with rows of colorful embroidery. They can also serve a practical purpose as pleats in a garment, holding in fullness.

Traditionally, pin tucks are formed by stitching very near a folded edge, but an easier method is to use a pin-tuck foot and a twin needle. The two needle threads share one bobbin thread, which pulls the fabric up between the rows of stitching. Twin-needle pin tucks are always even because the two rows of stitching are exactly parallel. The grooves under the pin-tuck foot keep multiple pin tucks the same distance apart.

Twin needles vary in size and are numbered, first, according to the distance (in millimeters) between the needles and, second, by the size of the needles. For example, a 2.0/80 twin needle indicates that size 80 needles are spaced 2 mm apart.

Consult your owner's manual or dealer about pin-tuck feet for your machine. They may come in more than one size. The narrower the grooves, the finer the pin tucks will be. Use a larger-grooved foot for pin tucks in bulkier fabrics. For stitching pin tucks, choose the twin needle size that most closely corresponds to the spacing of the grooves.

Twin-needle pin tucks require two spools of thread on top. To prevent the threads from tangling, place the spools so they unwind in opposite directions:

the left spool to unwind from behind, the right one to unwind from the front. Increasing upper tension slightly results in a more pronounced pin tuck.

To add decorative pin tucks to a garment, sew them into your fabric before you cut out the pattern. For closely spaced tucks, guide the previous tuck down one of the grooves in the pin-tuck foot. Experiment with spacing by using different grooves. To leave space for embroidery between tucks, use the edge of the presser foot as a guide. Work all pin tucks in the same direction to avoid distorting the fabric.

Pile fabrics, genuine or synthetic suede and leather, and quilted fabrics are among those that pose challenges at the sewing machine because they slip or stick to the presser foot. But the Even Feed foot makes these special fabrics as easy to sew as muslin.

With an all-purpose presser foot, fabrics slip during machine stitching because the feed dogs grab only the lower layer. Meanwhile, the presser foot simply pushes the upper layer against the lower layer. For most fabrics, slippage of the upper layer against the lower layer is only slight and can be controlled by pins. But even a small amount of slippage is obvious on a striped or plaid fabric that requires matching.

With feed teeth of its own, the Even Feed foot synchronizes the rate at which upper and lower layers of fabric feed under the needle. Sticky fabrics are not held back by the presser foot, because it "walks." Stripes that start out matched remain matched the entire length of a seam. Multiple layers can be machine-quilted without puckers, and stretchy velours stay together for smooth seaming.

A gathering foot is ideal for creating ruffles. It is fast and the ruffles are even, but you cannot adjust the gathers after stitching is completed, so the foot is not meant to gather a specific amount of fabric to fit into a section, such as a sleeve to a cuff. The gathering foot is great for home decorating projects that need yards of gathered fabric, if the fabric is not too heavy.

Four factors determine how much fullness will be produced:

• Fabric. Lightweight, fine fabrics gather more than heavier, more dense fabrics.

• Stitch length. The longer the stitch, the more fullness will be drawn into each stitch.

• Tension. The tighter the tension on the machine, the fuller the gathers will be.

• Machine operator. For even gathering, let the machine feed the fabric; do not hold it back.

Experiment with strips of the fabric you will use for your project. Place fabric under the gathering foot and begin sewing. Try different stitch lengths and tension settings until you achieve the fullness desired, and then record the machine settings used.

Using Special Accessories

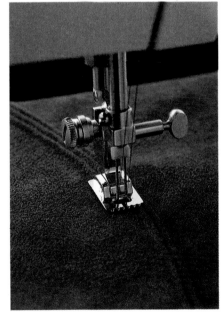

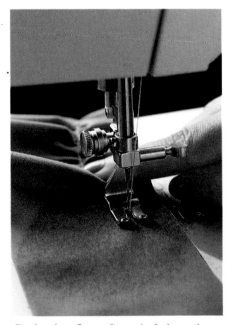

Pin-tuck foot and twin needle. Tighten tension slightly. Stitch, with right side of fabric up. Place first tuck under channel of pin-tuck presser foot; determine distance from the first tuck by channel selection. Stitch additional tucks.

Even Feed foot. Match stripes or plaids at beginning of seamline. Even Feed foot will keep them matched as you stitch seam.

Gathering foot. Set stitch length for long stitches; the longer the stitch, the greater the fullness. Tighten the tension. Hold index finger behind presser foot while stitching. Fabric piles up against finger. Release finger, and repeat.

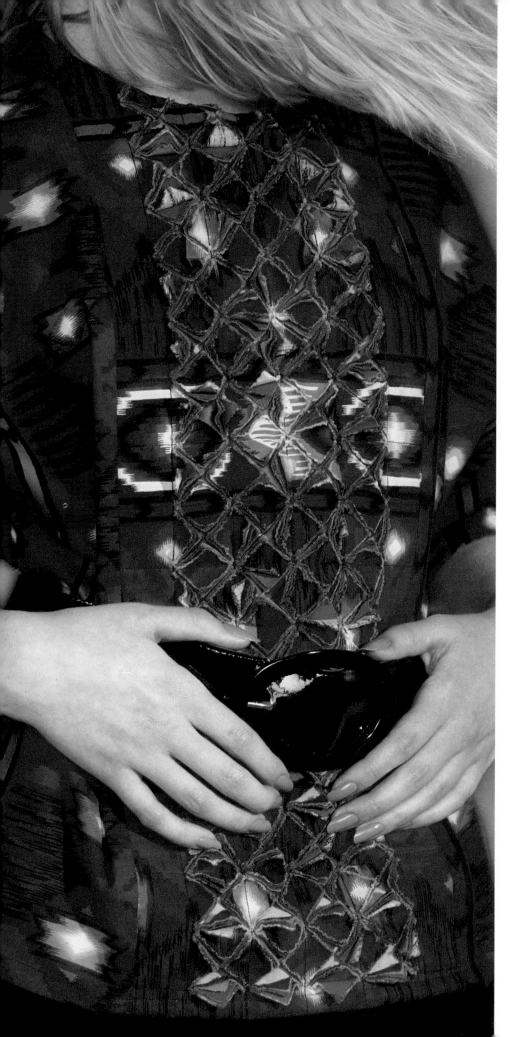

Surface Design & Embellishment

Many people sew to express their creativity: to make something unique, something enduring, something of quality. A very creative way to make a garment unique is to change or add to the surface. Embellishments added to the surface may be trim or appliqué, decorative snaps, or decorative stitching, to name a few. Other ways of changing the surface of a fabric or garment may be adding paint, piecing, or prairie points; pleating; or slashing through layers of fabric. This may be done to a section of the garment or to the fabric from which the garment will be made.

Surface design can make a simple garment or fabric exquisite and one-of-a-kind. When choosing a pattern or style for your surface design project, choose a simple pattern; one that will show off your surface design effort and not overshadow it. It may be easiest to start with an inset of the surface design, such as on the blouse on page 65 or on the tie on page 61. Or make a small project, such as the belt on page 61. Always practice with scraps of your fabric and embellishments, to learn the technique as well as to play with the color and design, before making final decisions. Designing an entire jacket or vest should be reserved for a later project, when you have more practice and skill.

Learn the technique with a good beginning project, such as a "blooming" fabric insert on a blouse.

Add appliqués, decorative snaps, eyelets, and trim to a jacket.

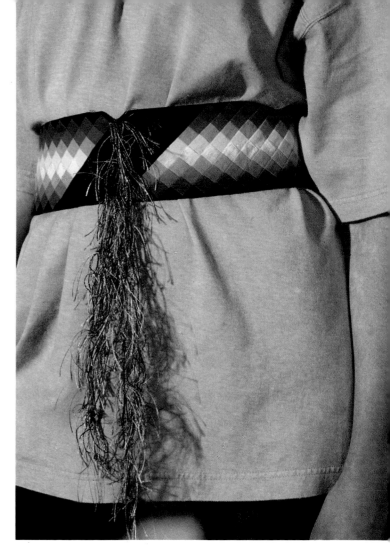

Start with a simple piecing project, such as a belt or tie.

Add sparkle or interest quickly and easily to a ready-to-wear or sewn garment.

Piecing

Piecing is sewing small sections of fabric together to create larger ones. It may be done by hand or machine. Scraps can be combined to create geometric shapes or pictorial scenes, or they may be assembled randomly. Several fabrics may be stacked and cut at the same time, using a rotary cutter and mat. This makes preparing the fabric for many traditional piecework patterns an easy job. Ethnic piecing traditions such as Seminole patchwork (page 62) also provide shortcut methods for creating pieced fabrics. A small pieced strip inserted diagonally into a belt or jacket front band, a miniature pieced "quilt" inserted into a man's tie, a randomly pieced jacket or vest are just a few ways piecing may be used to make a garment unique.

A "prairie point" is another form of piecing. It is a triangularly folded piece of fabric sewn into a seam. Prairie points seem to float on the surface of the fabric. They can add interesting textural and color punctuation to a pieced garment, accessory, or quilt.

How to Make a Prairie Point

Fold a strip of fabric in half lengthwise. Bring folded edges together at center. Press and trim the ends to form a triangle. Stitch into seam. Folded edges may face either up or down.

Necktie with a pieced insert can be made using a commercial pattern and choosing the piecing design and location.

Vest features a variety of piecing designs and prairie points for surface interest.

Pieced belt or waistband can tie an outfit together by coordinating colors from the garment or accessories.

Seminole Patchwork

The quick and easy strip-piecing techniques of the Florida Indians have traditionally been done on the sewing machine. Two of the Seminole patchwork patterns, checkerboard and diagonal, are shown below and can be made using a quick piecing technique. Seminole patchwork can be incorporated into vests, belts, and ties, or combined with other patchwork designs.

How to Sew a Seminole Patchwork Strip (checkerboard)

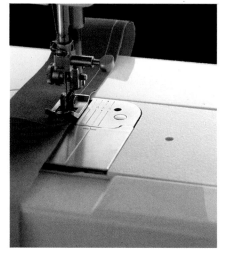  

1) Cut equal strips of two different fabrics on the straight grain. Stitch the strips together, using a 1/4" (6 mm) seam allowance. Press the seam to one side.

2) Cut pieced fabric perpendicular to seam, into strips the same width as the original. A see-through ruler and rotary cutter are helpful for this.

3) Arrange strips in a checkerboard pattern. Stitch together, using a 1/4" (6 mm) seam allowance; match center seams carefully. Press seams to one side.

How to Sew a Seminole Patchwork Strip (diagonal)

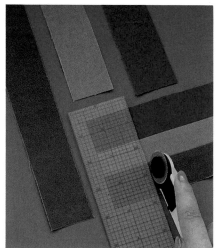  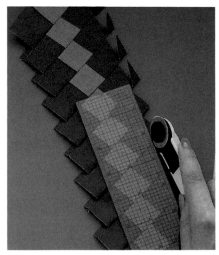

1) Cut equal strips of three different fabrics on the straight grain. Stitch together, press, and cut into strips as in steps 1 and 2, above.

2) Arrange strips so top of center stripe aligns with middle of center stripe on adjoining strip. Stitch, using 1/4" (6 mm) seam allowances. Press seams to one side.

3) Trim off points on raw edges to make the strip even.

Pleating

Pleats are formed by folding and pressing fabric. Some very interesting effects may be achieved with pleating on striped fabrics. An interesting striped fabric can be created by piecing fabric in gradations of color alternately with black as shown. Then the colored stripes are concealed within the pressed pleats. Where the pleats are released at hip level, the colors show with the slightest movement.

For any striped fabric, whether you buy it or piece it yourself, the width of the stripes determines the width of the pleats. Experiment to decide which colors to show and which to hide within the pleats. Pleats may be released from a seam or held in position at one end with edgestitching.

Lightweight wools, cottons, silks, and linens will pleat sharply. Select crisp, firm fabrics for garments with pressed pleats. Also, check to see if stripes are on the straight grain before buying a fabric; pleats will not hang properly if stripes are off grain.

Slashing

Slashing is a process of sandwiching and stitching together several layers of fabric, and then cutting through some of them in spots to expose successive layers. When washed, dried, and brushed, the cut edges curl and fray to create a richly textured surface. This technique can create colorful, textural effects, and is sometimes called "blooming."

Slashing may be done within a grid of rectangles or triangles, or between a series of lines. The fabrics may be layered as full-size pattern pieces, or as an insert for a yoke or other section of a garment. For inserts, bits and pieces may be sandwiched for interesting color variations and textural effects to pull an outfit together. Use tightly woven natural fiber fabrics, such as cotton.

Slashed panel of blouse is a good beginning project. Use colors in print fabric for inner layers.

How to Make Fabric "Bloom"

1) Cut six pieces of tightly woven 100 percent cotton according to pattern. Trim seam allowances off the four inner layers. Mark a grid of 1⅜" (3.5 cm) squares on top layer. Stack layers, matching seamlines; stitch together on marked lines.

2) Cut a ¼" (6 mm) slit in center of selected squares along diagonal, using seam ripper. Cut through any or all of the top five layers of fabric; do not cut through the backing layer. Clip from center to corners, using sharp scissors.

3) Wash and dry by machine to make the fabric "bloom." The more times you wash and dry it, the more fabric will bloom. If desired, brush surface with stiff brush to fray cut edges.

Appliqué, Embroidery & Beading

Appliqué, embroidery, and beading are three surface design techniques in which something is applied on top of a base fabric. Often, these techniques are combined to produce striking visual and textural effects on the surface of a garment.

Traditionally, appliqué, embroidery, and beading have been done by hand. Stunning results may also be achieved using the sewing machine. Special presser feet are available for most sewing machines for satin stitching, free-motion embroidery, and for applying braid, beading, and cording. Many threads, such as ribbon threads and embroidery threads, are designed for decorative stitching. The decorative stitches built into your sewing machine, used creatively with interesting threads, cording, and fabric combinations, can yield attractive results.

When planning a sewing project that includes appliqué, embroidery, or beading, be sure to consider the compatibility of your materials. For example, don't use invisible nylon thread to sew an appliqué to linen; the high heat necessary to press the linen will melt the nylon thread. Make sure your ribbon or yarn is colorfast if used on a washable garment. Thinking ahead about compatibility of all materials used and practicing these techniques on scraps will save time and trouble in the long run.

Another surface treatment for a finished garment, which can be used on its own or with other techniques, is painting the surface with fabric or puff paints. Paints can be spattered, sponged, or stamped, and some, such as puff paints, may be used directly out of the tube. A variety of fabrics, including leather, can be painted, but test the paint on scraps of the fabric or leather that you are using. Leather scraps, painted or unpainted, are great for appliqués or accessories.

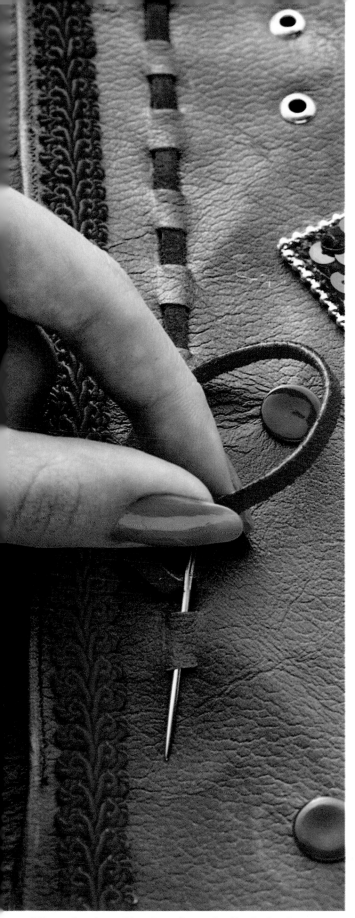

Glue on a sequin appliqué, and add a string of beads to the appliqué.

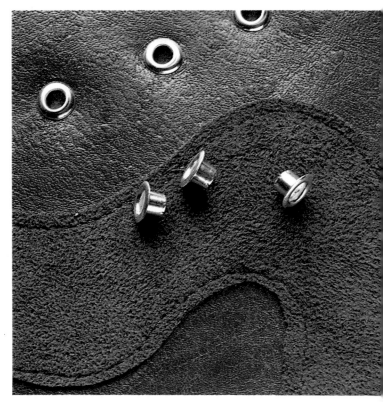

Thread strips of leather through slits in leather or suede, and add upholstery trim by hand. Apply decorative snaps for more interest.

Sew leather appliqués, using the straight stitch on your sewing machine, and add eyelets or snaps.

Adding Shine & Sparkle

A basic sweater can be turned into a glamorous evening option of understated elegance or glitzy shine. Or try the unexpected and add a lace that matches your black lace skirt to a cashmere sweater or cardigan. Add a touch of shine to a chiffon or georgette print scarf or blouse by outlining a predominant design motif with strings of tiny beads, rhinestones, or sequins. Or add these items to a tie or belt to finish a holiday outfit. Also, an appliqué from lamé can be added. Many times shine and sparkle can be worn in the daytime. Try some of these ideas on denim jackets and shirts.

Most of these trim items can be held in position with glue stick and tacked on by hand. Often there is a sewing machine foot, such as a beading foot, that can make the task easier.

Experiment with a variety of items and their design before deciding on the finished look.

Prestrung sequins, metallic braid, appliqué, and seed pearls make this soft sweater knit unique.

Softly draped blouse in rabbit hair jersey can be made into an evening outfit by adding metallic trim, tiny nailhead studs, and fake faceted jewels. Make a taffeta skirt to complete the outfit.

Color & Design for Quilting

Quilts keep us warm and give us beautiful visual images. It is a satisfying experience to plan, cut, piece, and quilt, but it is even more satisfying to design your own quilt from scratch and choose the best possible colors to interact on the surface of your quilt. We need to rely on our own design sense and experience plus training in design and color to give a feeling of confidence. We all have an inner sense of balance and placement, but for some it may take more time to make a decision. Have confidence in yourself; take time for the design process to work. At each step of the process, stop and look at your design. Display it where you will walk by it and look at it. You will make your decision after a bit of time.

A knowledge of basic color terms makes the process more understandable. The process of designing first a block and then a quilt can be simple. Start with one block design as shown opposite. When the block design has been chosen, as well as the values, the block placement needs to be decided (pages 74 to 75).

Both of these steps are very systematic, making the whole process nonthreatening.

Definition of Color Terms

Value is the degree of lightness or darkness of a color. Light values are tints, and dark values are shades.

Hue is the name of a color.

Tint is a hue with white added, yielding a color lighter than a pure hue.

Shade is a hue with black added, yielding a color darker than a pure hue.

Tone is a hue with gray added, yielding a color with a gray quality.

Intensity or saturation is the purity or grayness of a color, the relative brightness or dullness. Colors with strong intensity are nearer the pure hue, and colors of weak intensity are approaching a gray.

Complementary colors are colors directly opposite each other on the color wheel. Complementary colors give a strong contrast; when mixed together or placed side by side, they tend to gray each other.

How to Design a Quilt

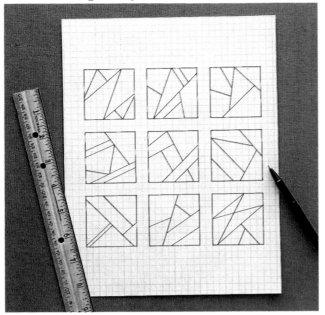

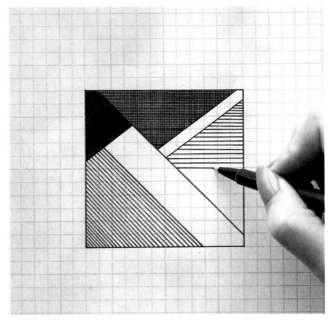

1) **Draw** a number of 2" or 3" (5 or 7.5 cm) squares on graph paper, with space between each square. Divide each square into six or eight areas.

2) **Choose** one or two of these designs to do a value study. It is too early to add color, as this introduces another element, so do your value studies using a black pen. You will have black and white as the strongest values, and by drawing lines (fine or heavy, close together or farther apart, and cross-hatching), you will get values of black, white, and gray.

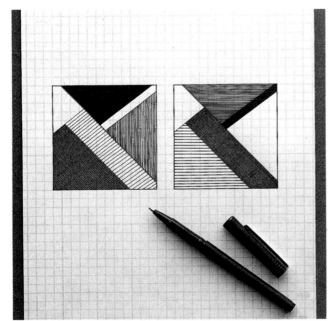

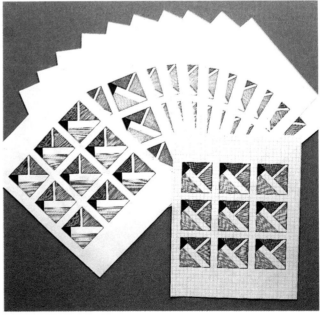

3) **Do** two or three value studies of the same design. The proportions of black, white, and gray change when the positions are rotated. The designs will look very different if black is placed in the largest shape and, on the next design, in the smallest shape. If the largest shape is solid black, it may overpower the design, especially at the next step in the designing process when the blocks are put together. From these value studies, choose one to work with.

4) **Draw** a page of the value study you chose, and photocopy it several times. Cut the designs apart, and work with these copies for the next step of the design process. This will save a lot of drawing time. The reproduction process distorts the image; therefore, use the copy as a designing tool, but go back to the original drawing when making templates.

Block Rotations

Until now the quilt block has been a single unit; now work in four-block units. Start by labeling one module as follows: A is the upper left corner, B is the upper right corner, C is the lower right corner, and D is the lower left corner.

After you have gone through the following steps, decide which block you like best and what size you want to make the block. Both the mirror image and the counterclockwise rotations work best with more divisions to the block.

1) Put the first four modules together the same way. The quilt top would then be formed with the units always in the same direction, with AB at the top.

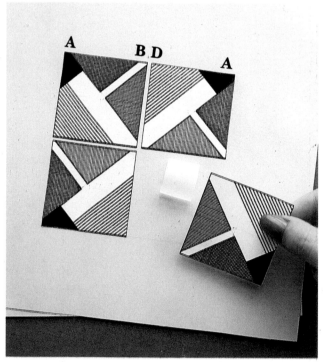

2) Start with AB at the top of the upper left module, and rotate the next module a quarter turn clockwise. DA is now at the top of the upper right module. Continue by rotating each module a quarter turn.

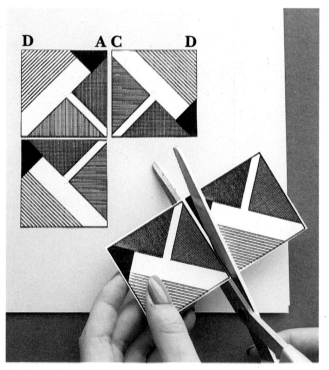

3) Start the block with DA at the top, and continue quarter rotations as in step 2.

74

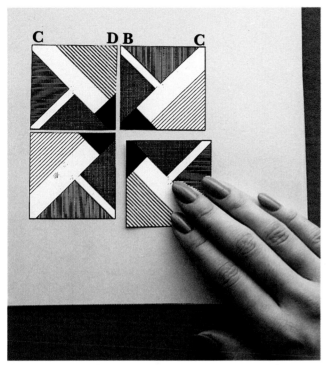

4) **Start** the block with CD at the top, and continue quarter rotations as in step 2.

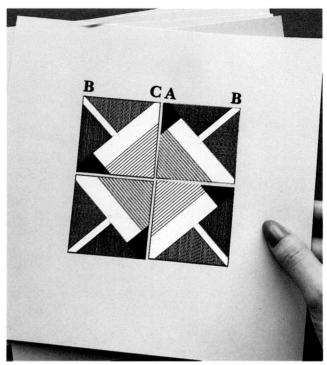

5) **Start** the block with BC at the top, and continue quarter rotations as in step 2. You now have five new versions of your quilt block. Your block is a four-block unit instead of a single unit. It also looks very different from the single module.

Reverse image. Put a mirror on the edge of your design. To draw this reversal, turn your original drawing face down, and take it to a light table or window. With the light coming through the paper, trace the design.

Counterclockwise rotation. To create another design variation, follow instructions for clockwise rotations, except rotate the modules counterclockwise.

English Smocking

The technique of smocking refers to gathering material into folds and creating designs by hand-stitching through one pleat at a time. It is used on many household items as well as on yokes, bodices, pockets, sleeves, and waistlines of clothing such as nightwear, children's wear, blouses, and dresses. There are many smocking stitches that allow for countless patterns and endless creativity, but with only two basic stitches many patterns can be created.

A decorative pattern results from the use of smocking. In addition, smocking gives shape to the garment. It provides an elasticity that pleats and tucks do not give. For smocking, a lightweight, crisp fabric is best. Lightweight polyester and cotton blends, batiste, broadcloth, calicos, or soft flannel are suitable because they will gather into pleats. Embroidery floss is used for the decorative stitching. A size 7 or 8 (55 or 60) needle is most often used with three or more strands of floss. Use a finer thread for batiste.

Smocking is done before the garment is constructed. The fabric should be preshrunk. The piece to be smocked should be at least three times larger than

the finished area, because smocking decreases the size of the fabric. If a desired commercial pattern does not use smocking, it may be adapted in a pattern with gathers. A basic pattern that involves a small area to be smocked will give best results. When you are working with two identical pieces such as collars, cuffs, or bodice fronts, it is helpful to complete them simultaneously to maintain uniformity.

Before the fabric is smocked, it must be gathered into pleats. A pleating machine may be preferred at this step to accommodate today's busy life-style. It provides a fast and efficient way of gathering the fabric. Since buying a pleating machine can be quite costly, one can simply take the fabric to a quilting store and have the piece pleated. The fabric is fed into the machine, which consists of 16, 24, or 32 needles. The needles are threaded with quilting thread because it is stronger, less likely to tangle, stays in the fabric better, and makes pleats that are fuller and more rounded. The result is evenly pleated fabric that is ready to be smocked. Before smocking, count the pleats, and mark the center so that symmetrical designs will balance.

76

The look of the finished pattern will depend on which stitch, or combination of stitches, is selected. A wide variety of stitches may be used. They are completed by working from left to right. Two of them are the cable stitch and the trellis stitch. The cable stitch is used often and is easy to learn. It is a compact stitch with a basket-weave appearance. The trellis stitch is versatile and can vary in the number of stitches that compose it. It gives a zigzag effect and can be worked to any height. Two pleats are worked at a time. Stitches are made in a steplike fashion.

The creativity involved with smocking comes into play during the planning of the design. Drawing a sketch of the design on paper before working on the fabric helps to eliminate uncertainty. Choose a dominant color for the theme, and use compatible colors or accent colors suitable for the fabric or design. Using dark, medium, and light colors enhances the design even further.

Pleating machine. Fabric is wound on a dowel, and the fabric end is inserted between two rollers. Fabric is fed through by turning a handle at the side of the machine.

How to Make a Cable Stitch

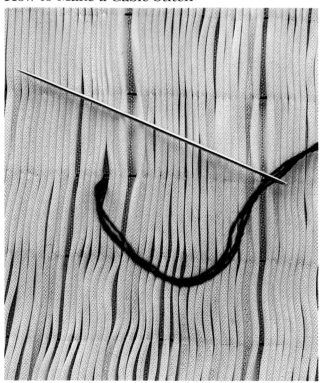

1) Bring the needle through the first pleat from the underside.

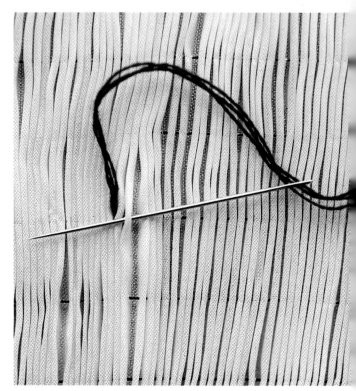

2) Place thread above the needle, and stitch under the second pleat.

How to Make a Trellis Stitch

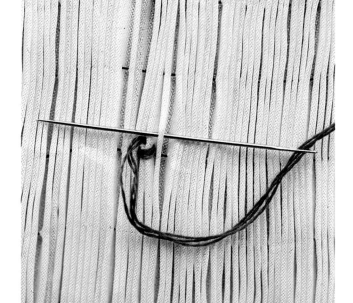

1) Start with bottom cable, bringing the needle through the first pleat from the underside. Placing thread below needle and moving up a quarter of the way between rows 1 and 2, stitch the next pleat.

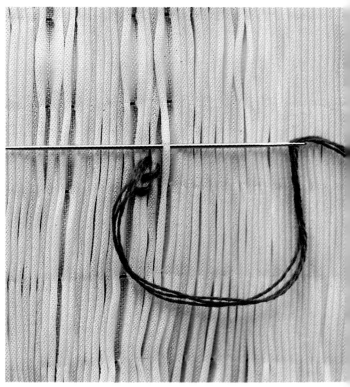

2) Keep thread below needle, and move up another quarter space to halfway point between rows 1 and 2; stitch the next pleat.

78

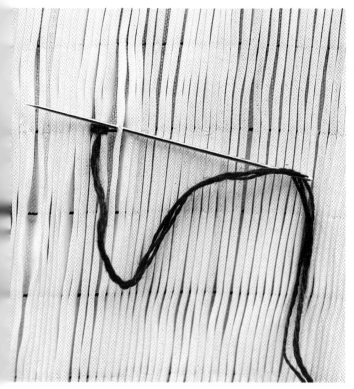

3) Place the thread below the needle, and stitch through the third pleat.

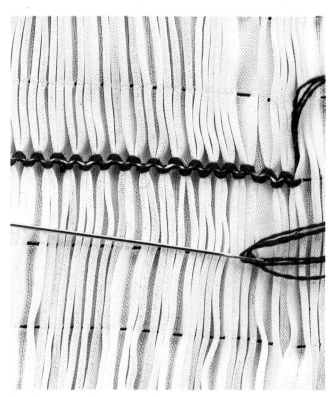

4) Alternate this way until the row is complete. Repeat the procedure for the remaining rows.

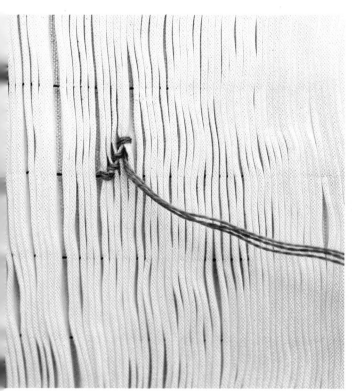

3) Place thread above needle, halfway between rows, and stitch the next pleat, making cable at top of trellis. This stitch completes first half of trellis.

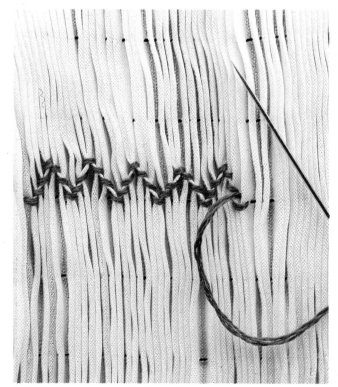

4) Keep thread above needle, and move down a quarter space; stitch next pleat. Repeat. With thread below needle, stitch the next pleat, making cable at bottom of trellis. Repeat steps 1 to 4 as necessary.

Smocked Christmas Ornament

Smocking can easily be used to make Christmas tree ornaments or decorative eggs, or be inset into a variety of projects, from home decorations to accessories. This 2" (5 cm) ornament is an excellent beginning project, because it is fast and easy.

Combinations of the two basic stitches on pages 78 to 79 can make a variety of patterns for your projects. Read pages 76 to 79 for basic smocking information.

YOU WILL NEED

Mediumweight fabric, 4½" × 22½" (11.5 × 57.3 cm).

Styrofoam® ball, 2" (5 cm).

12" (30.5 cm) satin ribbon, ¼" (6 mm) wide.

3" (7.5 cm) satin ribbon, ½" (1.3 cm) wide.

Embroidery floss and needle.

How to Make a Smocked Christmas Ornament

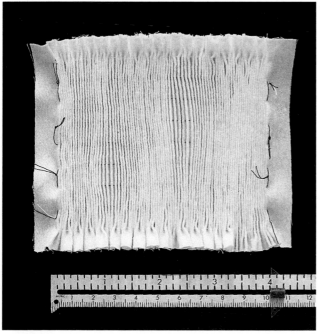

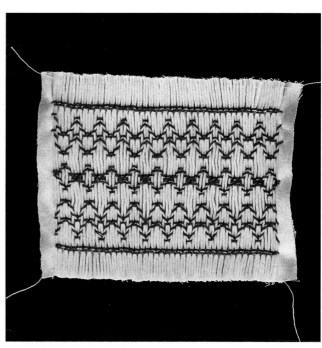

1) Pleat a piece of fabric 4½" × 22½" (11.5 cm × 57.3 cm) into 9 rows (page 77). Spread pleats to a width of 4" (10 cm). Tie the gathering threads into pairs with an overhand knot.

2) Smock pleated fabric (pages 78 to 79). Leave one pleat on each side for seam. Trim fabric ⅛" (3 mm) above gathering row 1 and below gathering row 9. Remove gathering threads from rows 2 to 8. (Other threads are used to pull rectangle into ball shape.)

(Continued on next page)

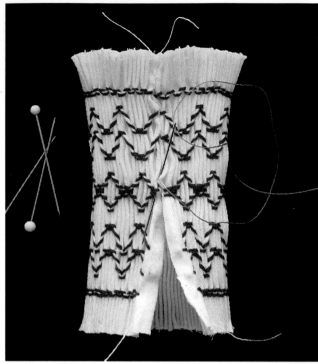

3) Turn under one side edge, matching smocking design. Pin and slipstitch. This makes a tube. (Pins were removed and contrasting thread was used to show detail.)

4) Slip Styrofoam ball into tube. Center design on ball and pull up gathering threads on rows 1 and 9, as tightly as possible. Clip threads.

5) Cut ⅜" (1 cm) ribbon into 9" (23 cm) and 3" (7.5 cm) lengths. Make 3 loops with 9" (23 cm) piece, and secure to top with a pin. Form loop with 3" (7.5 cm) piece for hanging, and pin to top with 2 decorative pins.

6) Use 3" (7.5 cm) piece of ⅝" (1.5 cm) ribbon to form a loop. Flatten loop, and pin to bottom of ball with 2 decorative pins.

Ideas for Smocking

After learning the smocking techniques and stitches on pages 76 to 79, you can make a variety of projects. Try the projects on this page, or create one of your own.

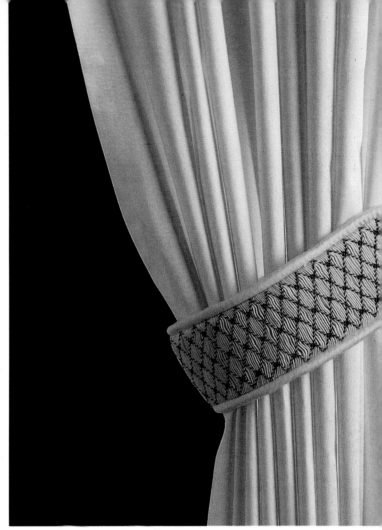

Beaded Christmas ornament is easy to do, using the cable stitch. Beads are added after the first stitch of a cable, as on page 78, step 1. Finish ornament, as in steps 3 to 6, opposite.

Smocked tieback with piping adds an original touch to this curtain.

Glasses case with smocked insert shows a new design using the cable and trellis stitches.

Rag Baskets

Rag baskets can be made by machine or by hand. Making rag baskets is a good way to use your stockpile of lightweight cotton or blended fabrics.

Try a basket in just one favorite fabric, or use a variety of fabrics. When choosing several fabrics, look for a mix of large and small florals, geometrics, stripes, checks, plaids, or tone-on-tone prints.

Cut fabric in 1" (2.5 cm) strips on the crosswise grain with rotary cutter or scissors, and ruler. When making a basket by machine, use a size 100/16 needle and a zigzag stitch. For making baskets by hand, use a size 85/13 tapestry needle. Use matching thread on either basket. The cording diameter can be varied on the hand-constructed basket (see You Will Need box).

Use your imagination in embellishing the baskets. Try large wooden or ceramic beads for handles. Wooden handles can be purchased and painted in coordinating colors. You can decorate your basket with woodland figures or silk flowers. Try a sprig of artificial holly for a Christmas basket. Heart-shaped or rectangular wooden bases, available in craft stores, will give your basket a different shape.

Use rag baskets as containers for mail, magazines, craft projects, jewelry, plants, fruit, guest towels, or nursery items. Construct flat coils for coasters, trivets, placemats, and rugs.

YOU WILL NEED

For machine-constructed basket:

Basket cording or clothesline, 1/4" (6 mm) diameter or less.

Lightweight cottons or blends.

For hand-constructed basket:

Basket cording, in 1/4", 1/2", or 3/4" (6 mm, 1.3 mm, or 2 cm) diameter.

Lightweight cotton or blended fabric; 1" (2.5 cm) strips for either narrow cording, or 1 1/2" (3.8 cm) strips for wider cording.

How to Make Machine-constructed Baskets

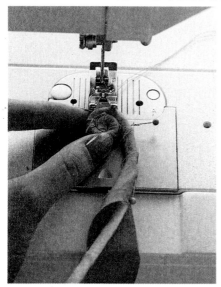

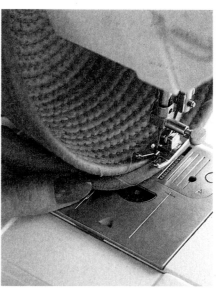

1) Cover end of cord with fabric strip, and wrap 5" to 6" (12.5 to 15 cm). Pin to hold in place. Bend into spiral shape, and zigzag together. For an oval basket or placemats, make your first turn 3" to 4" (7.5 to 10 cm) from the beginning.

2) Continue to turn and zigzag together until base is desired size. Turn work on edge, pressing base against machine to form sides. At the end of a fabric strip, start another; overlap previous strip. Splice cord, page 86, step 3.

3) Continue sewing until basket is the desired height. End by cutting cord and wrapping fabric slightly past end of cord. Stitch end to previous coil.

1) Taper end of cording with scissors. Thread tapestry needle onto a fabric strip. Take end of strip opposite from needle, and begin wrapping it tightly around cording about 5" (12.5 cm) from end. Wrap almost to end of cording. Bend end of cording to make a loop. Leave a hole in the loop. Wrap over both cords.

2) Start spiraling cord to form a circle. To fasten, insert the needle into the hole that was left and pull fabric firmly. Repeat. Construction now consists of wrapping the cording independently 2 or 3 times and then fastening to previous coil 2 or 3 times. Needle cannot pierce fabric, so find a spot where needle can go through.

3) Overlap new strip over end of previous strip. To splice cording, taper ends of old and new cords for about 4" (10 cm). Overlap the ends; wrap masking tape around the splice. Continue until bottom is desired diameter. Build up sides to desired height by laying cording on top of previous coil.

4) Add handles to last course of basket. Secure cord 3 or 4 times; wrap cord independently 5" to 6" (12.5 to 15 cm). Bend into handle shape. Secure to previous coil 3 or 4 times. Continue halfway around basket, and make second handle.

5) Finish basket by cutting cord at an angle and wrapping with fabric. Weave end of fabric in and out, and cut off.

Rug Braiding

A handmade braided rug is a decorative addition to a room. The manufactured braided rug will never equal the handmade rug in durability and beauty. It can be made in any size desired, from a small mat to a room-size rug. A variety of shapes can be braided: oval, round, square, rectangular, and heart. Patterns are often braided into a rug, and color schemes are planned in detail.

Select two or three colors from your room as the colors for your rug. Don't make the center a solid dark color; your rug will look like a target or a hole in the floor. Color changes should be made one strip at a time at the eleven o'clock position. A complete color change will take three rounds.

Braiding accessories greatly reduce the time spent creating these beautiful rugs. For example, Braid-Aid™ is a tool used for folding fabric strips.

Start with an oval rug as a beginner, because this shape is the easiest. Although the rug is reversible, it will have two distinct sides. Braid on the top side, and lace on the bottom side. The top side will be more colorful and will have a sculptured look. Keep the tension tight and even as you braid, and the rug will be durable enough to last for years.

The most durable rugs are made from 100 percent wool. Collect all your fabric before you start your project. Start by finding things in your own home; old woolen blankets, coats, suits, and scraps from sewing projects can be used. Also, a woolen mill that manufactures blankets or a company that makes coats may sell scraps.

Wash fabrics with warm water in a mild soap solution. They may be machine washed on gentle cycle and dried at low temperatures to preshrink and soften the fabric for easier braiding.

Cut the strips on the straight grain of the fabric to the desired width. The width is determined by the weight of the wool. The length of the center braid is determined by the planned size of your finished rug. It will be the width subtracted from the length of the rug; for example, a 2' by 3' (61 by 91.5 cm) rug will have a center braid of 1' (30.5 cm). When the center braid is the desired length, work a modified square corner; this puts a sharp turn in the braid.

The weakest part of your rug is the lacing. Never shake a braided rug. Don't hang the rug; hanging weakens the lacing. To vacuum, use the attachments and follow around, not across, the braids. To clean, use the same method you use for the rest of your carpeting. Very little water is needed; only the top surface needs to be washed. Professional cleaners who have experience cleaning braided rugs do an excellent job. If storing your rug, roll it up and wrap it in a sheet.

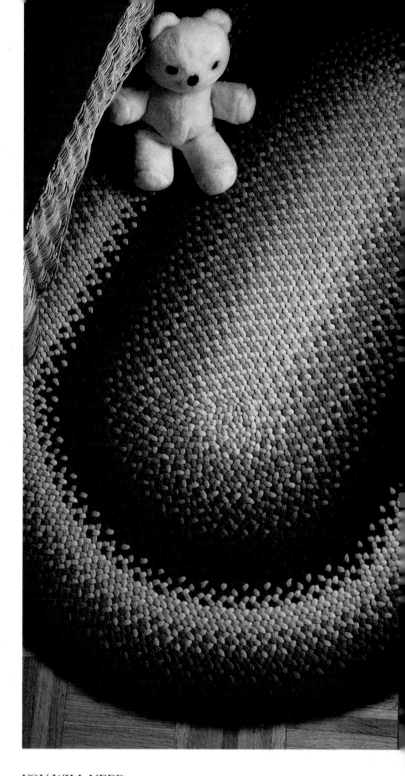

YOU WILL NEED

Strips of 100 percent wool fabric. A rug, 1' × 1' (30.5 × 30.5 cm) requires 1 yd. (0.95 m) or 1 lb. (0.45 kg) of fabric.

Braid-Aid™, a tool for folding strips into tubes (kit of 3).

Braidkin™, a curved bodkin needle used for lacing.

Linen thread, 3-ply for small projects and 6-ply for rugs over 6' × 6' (183 × 183 cm).

Rotary cutter or scissors; ruler.

How to Make an Oval Braided Rug

1) Begin by threading the strips into the Braid-Aids™. Join two of the strips with a bias seam. Trim and press open. (Use a bias seam for adding future strips.)

2) Attach the third strip to one side of the seam (T-start), with the opening to the right. For the first few inches (centimeters), hand stitching may be necessary to hold folds in place.

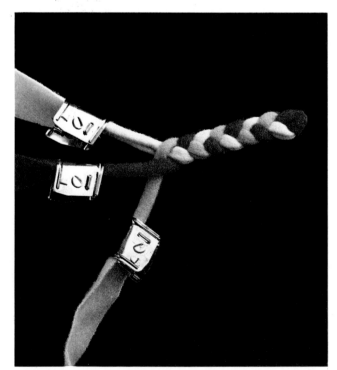

3) Braid right strip over center, left strip over center, and continue alternating strips in this order. Keep the opening to the right. Develop an even tension that is tight enough so you cannot separate the braids with your fingers. Work to desired length.

4) Make modified squared corner by numbering the strips from left to right: 1, 2, and 3. Work 1 over 2, 2 over 1, 3 over 2 tightly. Renumber strips from left to right, and repeat once.

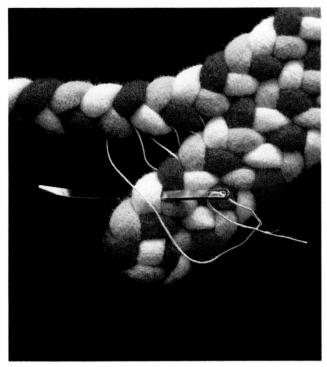

5) **Sew** two center braids together, starting at first bend and working around T-start; use a sharp needle and linen thread. Switch to bodkin needle. On the straight sides, lace every loop of rug and braid. On the curved ends, skip loops of braid only.

6) **Relace** if rug cups, skipping more loops of braid. Rippled edge indicates too many skipped loops. On the next round, skip fewer loops, and the problem will correct itself.

7) **Finish** rug by tapering each strip 5" to 7" (12.5 to 18 cm) on curve. Turn under the edge of each strip, and blindstitch together with matching thread.

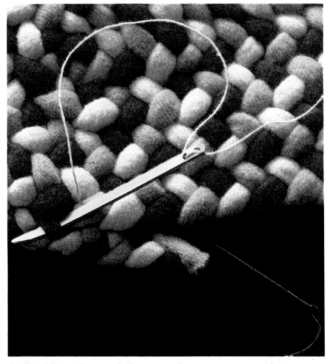

8) **Braid** to the end. Lace as far as you can, then back-lace several inches (centimeters), and cut the thread. Tuck end into loop, and blindstitch in place.

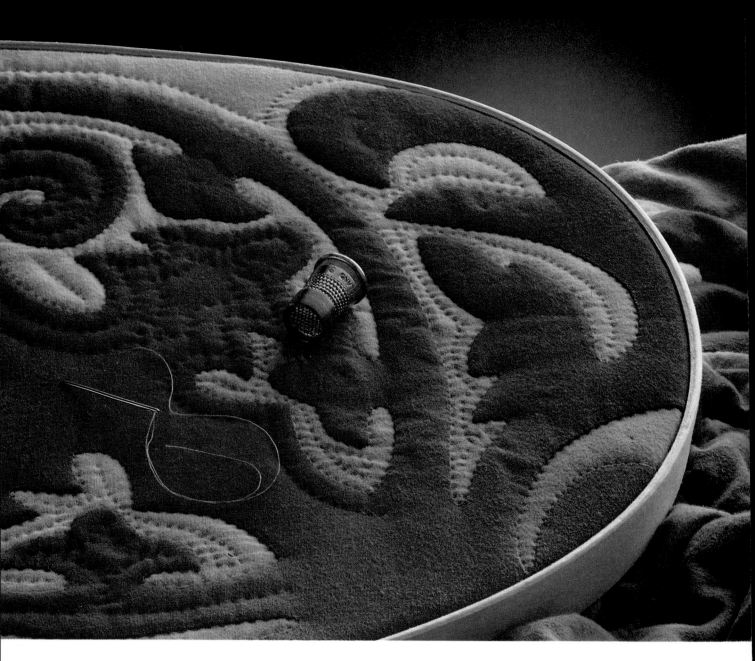

Hand Appliqué for Quilting

Appliqué is often perceived to be a tedious, time-consuming task. It takes time, but you can create any shape or form you desire within the limits of the technique. It can be realistic or abstract; the lines can be curved or straight. In a pieced quilt, most designs are based on straight lines, but in appliqué, most are based on curved lines. There is more freedom in hand appliqué. There are several different appliqué methods. In regular appliqué, several pieces are arranged to create a design; each piece lies directly on the background fabric, except for small areas where an edge of one piece might lie under another. In multilayered appliqué, several pieces lie one on top of the other, giving the design a three-dimensional look.

To make an appliqué quilt top, you will need a needle and thread, pins, scissors, markers, a well-padded ironing board, and a steam iron. Beeswax and a thimble are optional, but helpful. For Hawaiian and other large-motif quilts, you will also need shears. For quilts with motifs that are repeated, you will need to prepare templates for cutting pattern shapes.

Use a good-quality regular sewing thread. Match the thread to the color of the piece you are appliquéing. Work with a length of thread about 18" (46 cm) long. Longer lengths just get in the way and take too long to pull through the fabric, often creating small knots in the thread. And the more a thread is pulled through the fabric, the more it becomes worn, causing it to break. If the thread tends to tangle and break, try pulling it through beeswax.

Sew with the thinnest needle you can use comfortably. This may be a sharp or a between (a quilting needle), size 10 or 12.

Templates may be cut from plastic or other materials. Cut templates without seam allowances. Add a scant ¼" (6 mm) seam allowance to each piece of fabric when cutting it out. At first, you may want to mark seam allowances before you cut; with practice, you will be able to judge the correct seam allowance by eye and eliminate the marking step.

When marking around templates onto the appliqué fabric, use a sandpaper board under the fabric to keep the fabric and template from slipping, and to make a darker impression with the marker. Make a sandpaper board by gluing a piece of very fine wet/dry sandpaper to a stiff piece of cardboard, plastic, or ¼" (6 mm) plywood.

The best stitch to use for appliqué is the blindstitch. It virtually disappears into the fabric. If you can learn to work the blindstitch both toward and away from yourself, it can be a big help. Some pieces are easier to sew in one direction than the other. Take very small stitches when blindstitching. The smaller the stitch, the more control. Stitches ¹⁄₁₆" (1.5 mm) apart or less are recommended.

The heart is a classic design for learning appliqué, because it includes techniques for stitching straight edges, curves, and both inside and outside corners. Careful placement of pins, minimum seam allowances, and the needle-rolling technique, combined with the blindstitch, allow you to sew smooth edges with invisible stitches without basting.

How to Blindstitch a Heart Appliqué Using the Needle-rolling Technique

1) **Trace** outline of design lightly on background fabric. Trace design on right side of appliqué fabric, with straight of grain running through center. Cut out appliqué with scant ¼" (6 mm) seam allowance.

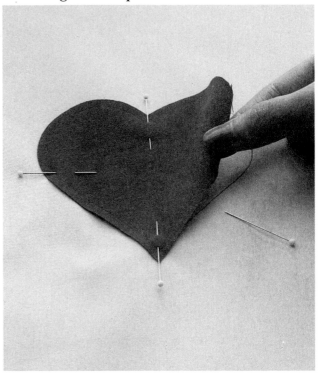

2) **Match** stitching line of appliqué to line drawn on background fabric; pin at top, bottom, and each side. Remove pin on straight edge; turn under seam allowance and repin through fold.

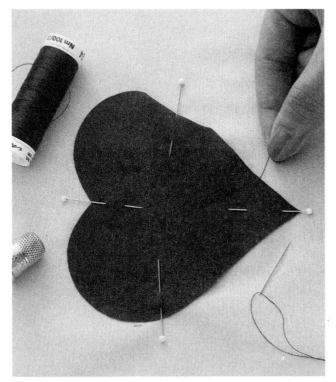

3) **Tie** knot at one end of thread. Bring threaded needle up through fabric from wrong side of appliqué slightly away from point at marked line. Knot will be hidden in fold.

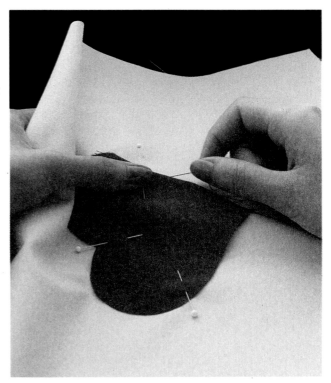

4) **Place** heel of hand on background fabric and hold pinned fold with other hand. Holding fabric taut, use tip of needle to roll under seam allowance to make a smooth line.

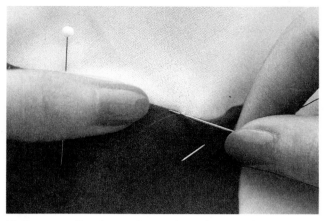

5) Put needle down through background fabric at edge of appliqué. Bring needle up into fold. Keep stitches small and needle parallel to edge of appliqué; pull thread snug. Blindstitch to pin.

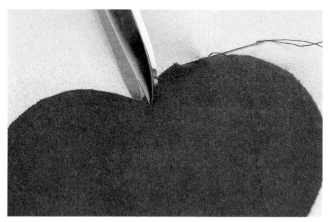

6) Pin fold on curve ½" (1.3 cm) from last stitch. Roll under seam allowance and blindstitch, as in steps 4 and 5. Continue stitching to top of curve. Clip to point. Stitch to ½" (1.3 cm) of inside point.

7) Pin folded edge just beyond clip. Roll under on marked line from pin to stitches, using a little tension from the needle; pull fabric taut so seam allowance will turn under smoothly.

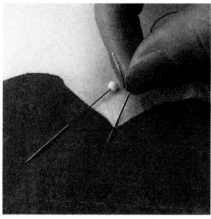

8) Stitch to point, rolling edge just beyond marked line at point; take two small overcast stitches. Stitch remaining curve in small segments.

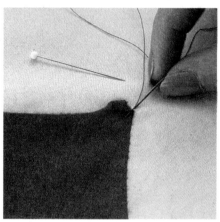

9) Blindstitch to outside point. Remove pin and take a small stitch. Fold seam allowance flat (90° angle) at the point. Take another stitch to secure point.

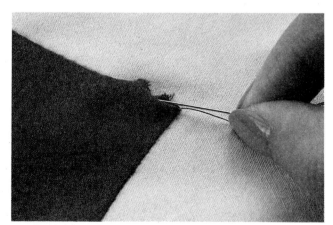

10) Use needle to pleat in seam allowance; this allows you to make a point half the width of the seam allowance. Tuck under remaining seam allowance; blindstitch.

11) End blindstitching by going over the same stitch three times on wrong side of background fabric under edge of appliqué. Run the thread under the appliqué; clip near surface.

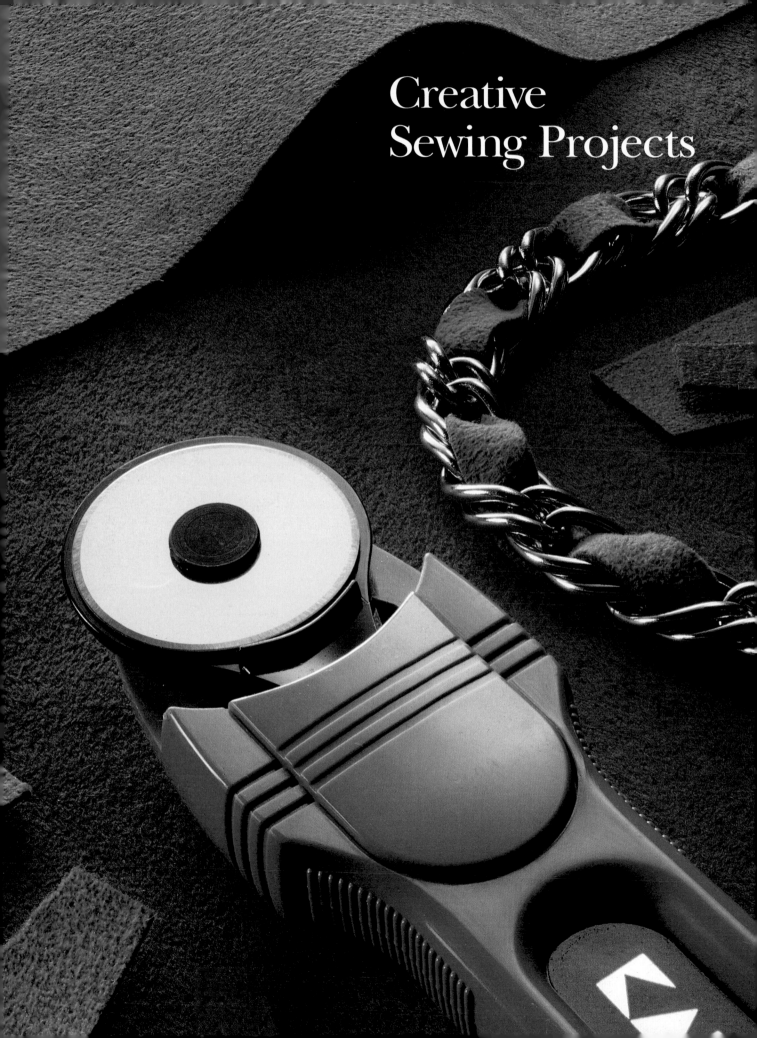

Creative
Sewing Projects

Creative Projects for You & Your Home

Making accessories for yourself or as gifts is an easy and fast way to express your creativity and practice some new skills. Accessories can make the difference between an ordinary outfit and a stunning one. Careful planning and designing helps in the long run. Use the scraps of your garment as inspiration for color and design. Use these accessory projects as a basis, and let your design ideas abound.

Sewing creative projects for the home makes your decorating unique. With only a few added touches or new design ideas and details, the ordinary can become special.

Handbags are a good way to coordinate an outfit. Use the inset as a way to introduce new design ideas.

Designer belts put the finishing touch on a special outfit. The belt can be matching or contrasting and the buckle covered in a variety of ways.

Scarves can be finished quickly and easily, by machine or by hand, for a professional appearance.

Comforter cover made from bedsheets is an attractive, easy way to protect a comforter or duvet.

Bed skirt with clustered gathers and double-flange pillow shams in a coordinating fabric can dress up a master bedroom or guest room.

Slipcovers for folding chairs and a reverse roll-up shade can spruce up a porch or add a finishing touch to any room.

Handbag with Inset

A creative accessory, such as a clutch, can be the final touch to make a special garment complete. Even the most expensive garment will improve with the addition of accessories. It is easy to coordinate accessories, especially if you have made the garment; you can use scraps of the same fabric or use a design or color from a print fabric.

The cost of ready-made accessories can quickly go over any wardrobe budget. Yet the cost of materials to make accessories is minimal, and you need not be an expert sewer. Find just the right color and fabric for making accessories. You may want to shop for accessory materials when you shop for the fabric and notions for your garment.

This elegant synthetic suede handbag may sell in a boutique for $100, but can be created for far less and can be made in the exact color and style you want. The bag shown, with finished dimensions of about 12¼" × 8¼" (31.2 × 21.2 cm), is only a beginning. Have fun piecing together synthetic suede scraps, stitching a monogram, or combining synthetic suede with snakeskin. Any fabric or design you wish can be used as the inset. Create the bag with an original design, making your own pattern (opposite).

✄ Cutting Directions

From fleece and fusible web, cut two rectangles each, 13½" × 9" (34.3 × 23 cm).

From synthetic suede, cut one rectangle 13½" × 9" (34.3 × 23 cm), three pieces using the pattern (opposite), two facing strips 13½" × 2" (34.3 × 5 cm), and two casing strips 11" × 1" (28 × 2.5 cm).

From lining fabric and interfacing, cut two rectangles each, 13½" × 7½" (34.3 × 19.3 cm).

YOU WILL NEED

12" (30.5 cm) metal snap-close frame, available at fabric stores or by mail.

¼ **yd. (0.25 m) synthetic suede.**

Snakeskin or scraps of synthetic suede, or any fabrics desired, for inset.

¼ **yd. (0.25 m) each of lining,** fleece, fusible web such as Wonder-Under™, and interfacing.

Glue stick or basting glue; thread.

How to Make a Pattern for Handbag Inset

1) **Draw** and cut rectangle, 13½" × 9" (34.3 × 23 cm), from paper. Draw design lines for inset, as shown. Finished inset piece is about 2½" (6.5 cm) wide. This design may be any shape or size desired.

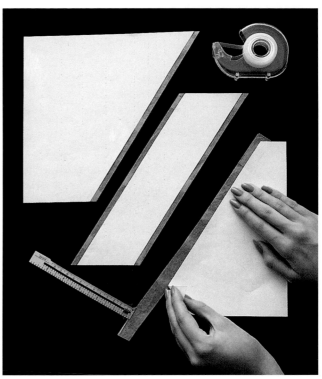

2) **Cut** pattern apart on drawn design lines. Add ¼" (6 mm) seam allowances to by adding strips of tissue paper extending ¼" (6 mm) design lines.

3) **Cut** inset pattern piece from snakeskin or desired inset fabric, and the two larger pattern pieces from synthetic suede.

4) **Place** synthetic suede and inset fabric right sides together; stitch, using ¼" (6 mm) seam allowances. Finger-press seam allowances to suede side. Topstitch suede, close to edge.

How to Make a Handbag

1) Fuse fleece to wrong side of the bag pieces by sandwiching fusible web between fleece and bag. Fuse only the suede, since snakeskin may melt with too much heat. Fuse interfacing to wrong side of lining. (Test any handbag materials to make sure they can tolerate heat needed for fusing.)

2) Center casing strips on suede facing strips, and secure with glue stick along long edges only. Topstitch each long edge, backstitching at each end. Stitch a facing strip to each bag piece, right sides together, with ¼" (6 mm) seam allowance. Trim away fleece at top of bag front and back. Stitch long edges of lining pieces to each free edge of suede facing strip.

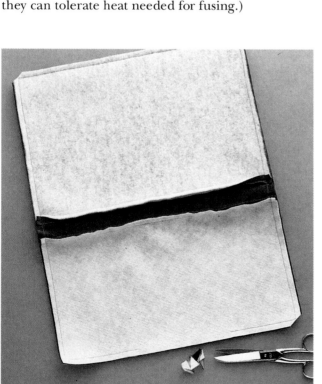

3) Align the two rectangles, right sides together, matching seams. Stitch, leaving a 5" (12.5 cm) centered opening at base of lining; clip corners. Turn right side out; slipstitch opening.

4) Fold lining seam allowances to inside; match side seams, and topstitch top edge ¼" (6 mm) from edge. Smooth lining to inside. Remove metal pins from ends of frame, and insert frame in casing. Replace pins.

Handbag Ideas

Strip-pieced inset (above) adds color to a synthetic suede bag. Thread a strip of fabric through chain for a coordinated look. Ribbon inset (right) gives texture and shine to this evening clutch. Twin-needle topstitched inset (below) gives a tailored look.

Designer Belts

Many ready-to-wear belts can be copied in synthetic suede, which can be purchased by the inch (centimeter), making it very economical. A small amount of 45" (115 cm) synthetic suede is adequate for waist sizes up to 40" (102 cm), depending on the style of belt. A snakeskin-covered buckle or purchased buckle added to a strip of synthetic suede makes a unique and easy belt to complete an outfit. Snakeskin scraps and a buckle kit transform synthetic suede into a luxurious belt; or cover the buckle with matching synthetic suede.

YOU WILL NEED

Synthetic suede, 3" (7.5 cm), depending on the width of the belt and for waists up to 40" (102 cm).

Buckle kit or purchased buckle.

Snakeskin scraps for buckle kit, optional.

Tips for Covering Buckles

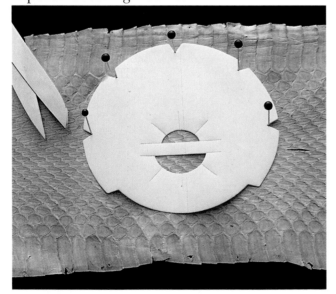

Snakeskin. Avoid any blemishes on skin. Snakeskin has a nap, so position skin so buckle feels smooth when worn. Insert pins at notches to mark position on wrong side. Follow manufacturer's instructions to affix snakeskin.

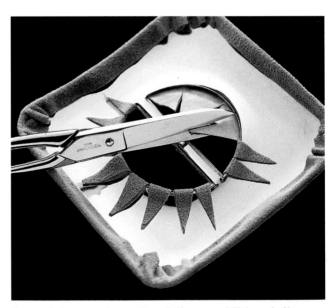

Smooth inner edges. Carefully cut additional slits on inner edges of buckle opening before affixing suede or snakeskin to buckle shape.

How to Make a Crushed Synthetic Suede Belt

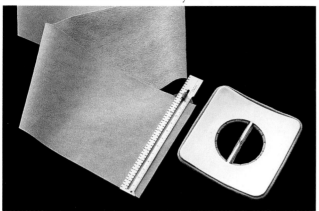

1) Measure length of center bar of buckle. Double this measurement and add ¾" (2 cm) to determine cut width of belt. Cut synthetic suede to determined width, with length equal to waist measurement plus 14" (35.5 cm).

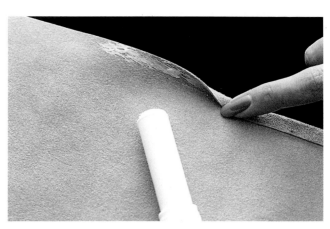

2) Apply glue stick along underside of one long edge. Fold over ⅜" (1 cm) and finger-press in place. Repeat for other long edge.

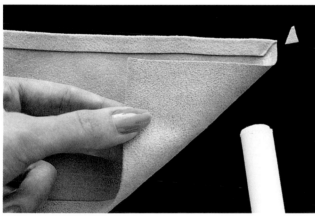

3a) Angled end. Position belt horizontally, wrong side up. Trim seam allowance diagonally at upper right corner. Apply glue stick along end. Fold end to meet long edge at top, forming 45° angle. Finger-press in place.

3b) Pointed end. Fold one end of belt lengthwise, right sides together. Stitch ¼" (6 mm) seam on short end. Apply glue stick to hold, and turn end right side out.

4) Topstitch ½" (1.3 cm) from folded edges, pivoting at corners.

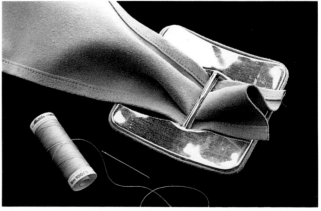

5) Wrap remaining end around center bar of buckle (do not use prong), with end extending about 2" (5 cm). Try belt on to determine the exact finished length. Secure loose end by hand or machine.

Scarves

Scarves are easy to make, and they complete ensembles, from blue jeans to a cashmere jacket to an evening suit. A first-time sewer can complete a fringed scarf or muffler easily or, with the help of a rolled hem on the overlock machine or serger, make a professionally finished silk or rayon scarf. For a silk or rayon scarf, use a lightweight to mediumweight soft woven fabric. If you are using the serger to roll the edges, choose a lightweight fabric. Use a metallic holiday fabric for a rolled hem scarf, or make a soft wool muffler for everyone on your gift list. You can make four mufflers with 1¼ yards (1.15 m) of fine, 60" (150 cm) wool.

✂Cutting Directions

Wool muffler: Straighten ends by pulling a cross thread and trimming evenly along pulled threads. Draw cutting lines on fabric, 15" (38 cm) apart, parallel with selvages. Cut four strips, each 15" × 45" (38 × 115 cm).

Silk or rayon square scarf: Cut a 36" or 45" (91.5 or 115 cm) square, depending on fabric width. Make sure threads are on the straight grain.

YOU WILL NEED

Wool muffler: 1¼ yd. (1.15 m) of 60" (152.5 cm) wide fabric (makes 4 scarves).

Silk or rayon square scarf: 45" (115 cm) of 45" (115 cm) wide fabric or 1 yd. (0.95 m) of 36" (91.5 cm) fabric.

How to Make a Wool Muffler

1) Zigzag with a short, narrow stitch close to each long edge and across each short end at top of desired fringe depth.

2) Fringe short ends by pulling away cross threads up to stitching.

How to Make a Silk or Rayon Square Scarf

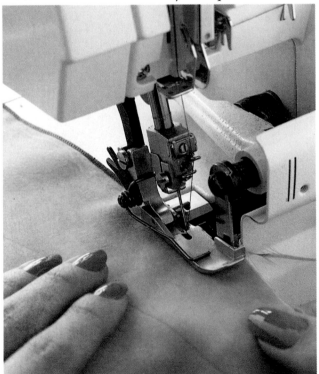

Square scarf with rolled hem. Set serger for rolled hem and finish all four edges of scarf. Fray-check each corner of scarf.

Square scarf with fringed edge. Pull threads to create fringe. A ¼" (6 mm) fringe on silk or rayon is more desirable because it doesn't add weight.

Sew a Comforter Cover from Sheets

A comforter or duvet cover is a removable sheet or fabric casing that protects your comforter and gives you the option of changing the look of a bedroom as quickly as changing your sheets. In less than an hour, with two flat sheets, you can make an envelope-style cover to custom-fit your comforter. Select a sheet with a decorative border, and use the border to

your advantage. It eliminates stitching on one end and quickly provides a custom trim. Before cutting, consider sheet design if matching stripes, plaids, or other designs. The finished cover size is 2" (5 cm) narrower and 2" (5 cm) shorter than the comforter to give a snug, puffy fit. Use another top sheet to make coordinating shams for your pillows.

YOU WILL NEED

Comforter Size	Sheets	Hook and Loop Tape	Plastic Rings	Ribbons
Twin	2 twin flats	7" (18 cm)	6	3 yd. (2.75 m)
Full	2 full flats	9" (23 cm)	6	3 yd. (2.75 m)
Queen	2 queen flats	11" (28 cm)	10	5 yd. (4.60 m)
King	2 king flats	13" (33 cm)	10	5 yd. (4.60 m)

How to Sew a Comforter Cover from Sheets

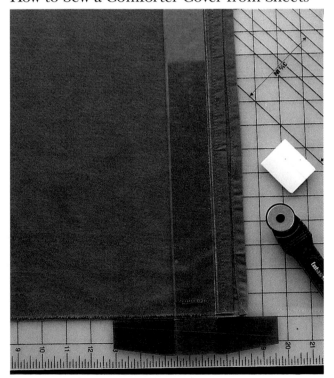

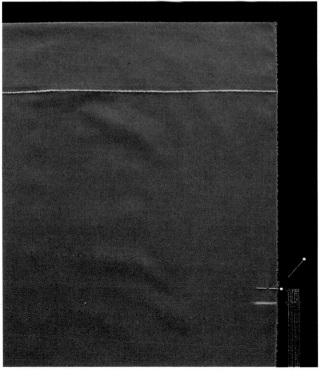

1) Cut both sheets 1" (2.5 cm) wider than finished cover width. With bordered edges even, fold one sheet in half lengthwise, aligning side edges along a straight edge. Square, mark, and trim lower edge.

2) Measure from squared lower edge to finished cover length; add ¾" (2 cm), and mark with pin on both sides.

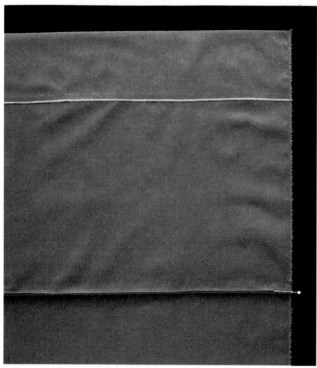

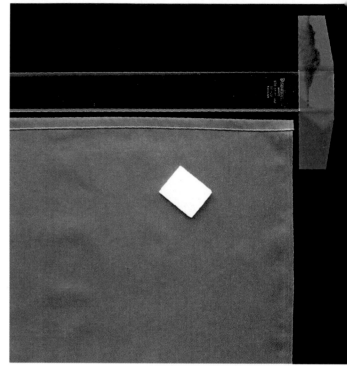

3) Fold sheet crosswise at pins, right sides together, and press. Stitch ¼" (6 mm) from fold. Fold again at stitching line, *wrong* sides together. This is the flap and back of cover.

4) Square, mark, and trim second sheet. For designed sheet, square end that continues flap design. Press under ½" (1.3 cm) twice, and stitch. This is the front of the cover.

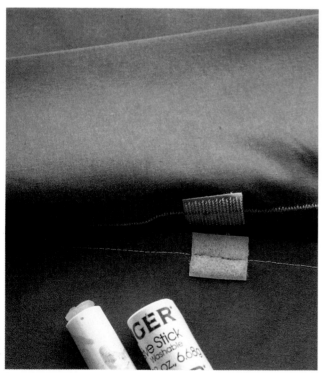

7) Glue 1" (2.5 cm) piece of hook side of tape to stitching line at marks on wrong side of flap. Glue 1" (2.5 cm) piece of loop half of tape to right side of front on hem edge at marks. Stitch through center of each tape; backstitch at each end.

8) Reverse flap, and pin to cover back, right sides together. Pin cover front to back, right sides together, lining up lower edges. Stitch ½" (1.3 cm) from raw edges around three sides of cover; finish raw edges.

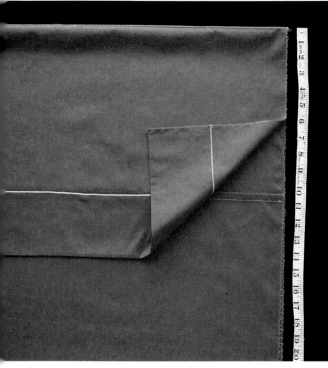

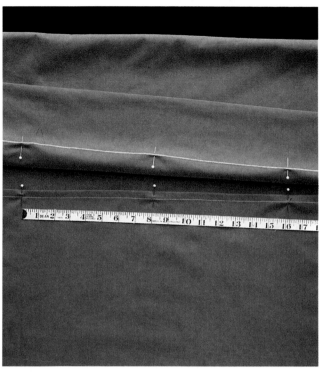

5) Place stitched hem of front under stitching on flap, and pin. Measure from upper edge to finished cover length, and add ½" (1.3 cm). Square, mark, and trim lower edge.

6) Mark placement for hook and loop tape on hem of front and stitching line of flap. Starting at the center, mark every 8" (20.5 cm).

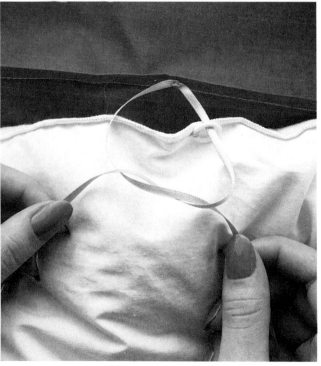

9) Stitch rings to corners and center of upper and lower edges of comforter. For queen or king size, use two more rings, evenly spaced.

10) Tack center of 18" (46 cm) ribbons to matching areas on seam allowances of cover. Turn right side out. Insert comforter. Tie ribbons through rings to prevent shifting of comforter.

Bed Skirt with Clustered Gathers

This attractive bed skirt consists of soft clusters of gathers at each corner of the bed and along the sides and foot. It is a good style for master bedrooms, since it combines the tailored look of a box-pleated skirt with the softness of a gathered skirt. Make it in a rich cotton chintz for a dramatic look, or in a wide eyelet with an embroidered, scalloped hem for a light and airy touch. Or use flat sheets that coordinate with the rest of your bedding for a total look that is less expensive to sew. Consider fabric weight as you plan your bed skirt. The heavier the fabric, the less dense the gathers. Lightweight fabric is easiest to work with. You may want to make the matching pillow shams (page 114) to complete the ensemble.

✂ Cutting Directions

Measure drop (from top of box spring to floor), width, and length of box spring. Cut depth of bed skirt is drop plus 2¼" (5.6 cm); this allows for ¼" (6 mm) clearance at the floor. Cut length of bed skirt is two times the length plus width plus 25" (63.5 cm) for each cluster of gathers: one in each corner, two on each side, and one (two for king-size bed) at the foot. Twin, full, and queen-size beds will need nine clusters of gathers; king-size, ten clusters. Seams should be calculated to fall at the beginning or the end of a gathered section.

Gathers are attached to the deck, the part of the bed skirt that goes on top of the box spring. Cut the deck 1" (2.5 cm) wider and 1" (2.5 cm) longer than the box spring.

YOU WILL NEED

Decorator fabric or sheets.

Flat sheet for bed skirt deck (twin-size for twin, full, or queen bed; full-size for king bed).

How to Sew a Bed Skirt with Clustered Gathers

1) Cut deck. Fold fabric in half lengthwise, then crosswise, so all four corners are together. Cut through all four layers to curve corners, using a saucer as a guide.

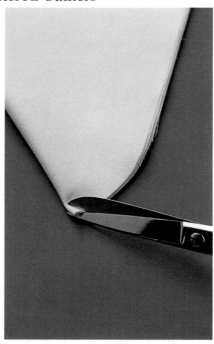

2) Fold curved corners in half to determine centers. Cut a notch through all layers at center line.

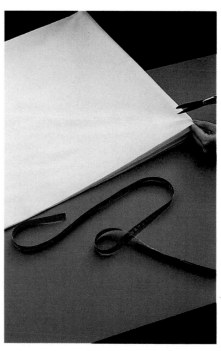

3) Fold the deck in half lengthwise and then into thirds. Notch deck sides at folds on cut edges, through layers, to mark placement for clustered gathers.

(Continued on next page)

4) Fold the deck lengthwise, in half for twin, full, or queen; in thirds for king. Notch deck foot at folds on the cut edges through layers to mark placement for clustered gathers.

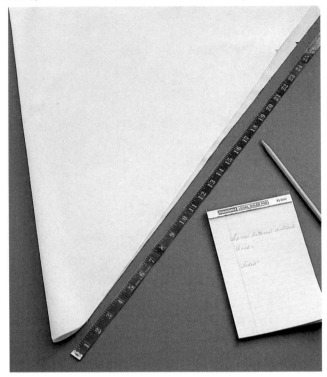

5) Measure and record distance between notches in deck. The spaces between notches at the foot may not be exactly the same as spaces between notches at the sides.

6) Cut skirt pieces. Position seams at beginning or end of gathering spaces. Mark adjacent seams in seam allowances.

7) Stitch skirt sections together to form one length, using ½" (1.3 cm) seam allowances; finish edges. Stitch double-fold 1" (2.5 cm) hem on lower edge; stitch double-fold ¼" (6 mm) hems on side edges.

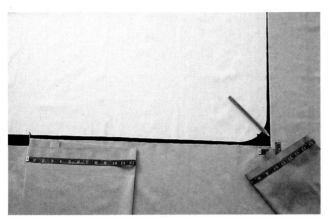

8) Mark placement of gathers on skirt according to measurements in step 5, opposite; begin at center of foot section. Hide any variation in measurement within gathers. Mark vertical stitching lines from upper edge to middle of bed skirt at each gathering placement mark.

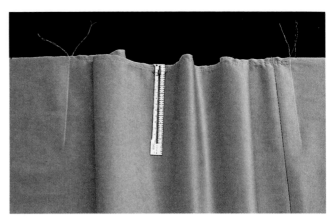

9) Stitch two rows of bastestitching or zigzag over a cord between the vertical marks in the spaces to be gathered. Stitch within ½" (1.3 cm) seam allowance.

10) Pin each gathered section along marked vertical lines, wrong sides together. Stitch along markings from upper edge to center, except at corners. At corners, stitch from upper edge for ¾" (2 cm) only.

11) Pull gathering threads to gather tightly. Center, flatten, and pin each cluster of gathers to skirt edge. Baste across gathers to secure.

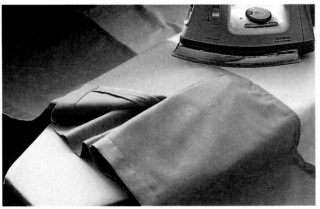

12) Pin skirt to deck, matching notches to center of gathers; stitch. Serge or zigzag edges around entire deck. Press seam allowances toward deck.

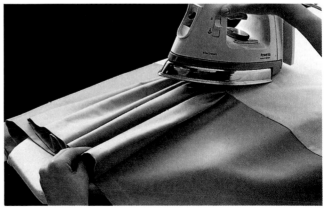

13) Steam each gathered cluster, to create soft vertical folds.

Double-flange Pillow Sham

To coordinate with the bed skirt (page 111), make a matching sham with gathers clustered at the corners. Border the sham in a single or a double flange; select fabrics to highlight colors and patterns in the rest of your bedding. A row of solid-colored piping adds a professional-looking finishing touch. If you use sheets for the bed skirt, you might make the pillow flange from the contrasting border or ruffles that often finish the top of a flat sheet. Or use lace or eyelet trim with a prefinished edge for the narrow upper flange, and fabric for the lower flange.

For the flanged sham, consider fabric weight. The flange fabric should have enough body to stand out from the sham, but the more layers and weight, the harder

it will be to gather the fabric tightly in the corners. One way to eliminate some bulk on a sham is to use a single layer of fabric for one or both of the flanges, finishing the edges with a narrow or rolled hem.

YOU WILL NEED

Decorator fabric to coordinate with bed skirt, if desired.

Zipper, about 3" (7.5 cm) shorter than length of sham.

Welting, 5/32" (3.8 mm) wide.

✂ Cutting Directions

For sham front, cut fabric 1" (2.5 cm) wider and 1" (2.5 cm) longer than pillow. For sham back, cut fabric 1" (2.5 cm) wider and 3" (7.5 cm) longer than pillow.

For each flange, cut two strips of fabric: cut length of each strip is equal to length plus width of cut sham front plus 15" (38 cm), and cut width is equal to two times finished width of flange plus 1" (2.5 cm).

Suggested finished width of lower flange is 4½" (11.5 cm), and suggested finished width of upper flange, 3½" (9 cm); lower flange should be 1" (2.5 cm) wider than upper flange.

For each sham, cut welting strip 1½" (3.8 cm) wide, by two times the length plus two times the width of pillow, plus extra for joining. Cut 5⁄32" (3.8 mm) cording the same length as welting strip.

How to Sew a Double-flange Pillow Sham

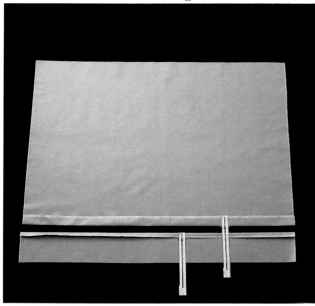

1) Cut a 3½" (9 cm) zipper strip from one long edge on sham back. Serge or zigzag one long edge of strip and sham back. Press under 1" (2.5 cm) on finished edge of back and ½" (1.3 cm) on finished edge of strip.

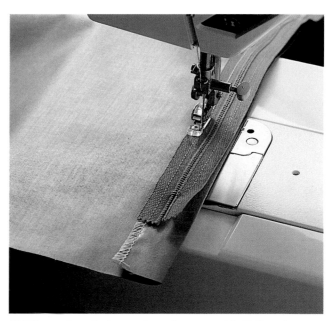

2) Place closed zipper face down on 1" (2.5 cm) seam allowance, with edge of zipper tape on fold. Using zipper foot, stitch inside edge next to zipper teeth, backstitching at each end.

3) Turn right side up. Place pressed edge of zipper strip along edge of teeth on other side of zipper. Stitch close to edge.

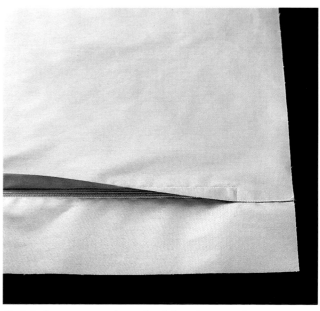

4) Stitch across each end of the zipper; pivot, and continue stitching through all layers to side edges.

(Continued on next page)

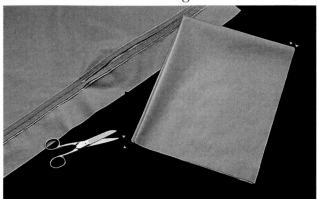

5) Fold sham front and back in half; fold again to quarter. Mark fold lines at center of each side edge with a notch. Open zipper partway.

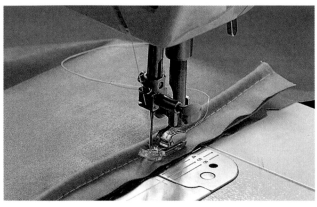

6) Center cording on wrong side of welting strip; fold strip over cording, aligning raw edges; stitch close to cording, using zipper foot. Place welting on right side of sham front, with end of cording ½" (1.3 cm) from center of lower edge and with raw edges even. Stitch scant ½" (1.3 cm) seam, beginning 2" (5 cm) from end of strip.

7) Clip seam allowance of welting strip as needle approaches each corner. Turn corner, with needle down through all layers. At each corner, hold layers at previous corner and pull gently so cording slips back into position.

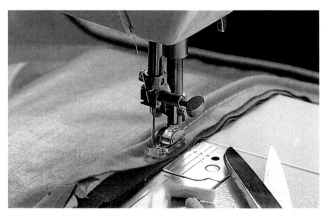

8) Stop stitching 4" (10 cm) from starting point. Trim cording and welting strip, allowing ½" (1.3 cm) for seam allowance. Remove stitching from welting ends. Stitch ends together. Finger-press seam open. Butt cording; finish stitching welting to sham front.

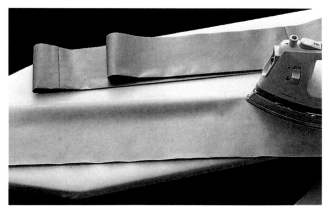

9) Stitch ends of each flange together to form two continuous loops. Press seams open. Fold in half lengthwise, with wrong sides together and raw edges even; press.

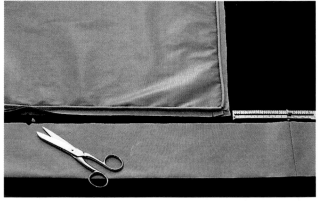

10) Align one flange with long edge of sham front so seamline of flange is 3½" (9 cm) beyond cut edge of sham front. Cut a notch in flange opposite notch in sham. Repeat for remaining flange.

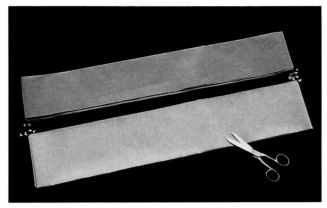

11) Fold flange at notch. Cut a notch at opposite fold line. Fold flange in half again to quarter; notch fold lines. Repeat for remaining flange.

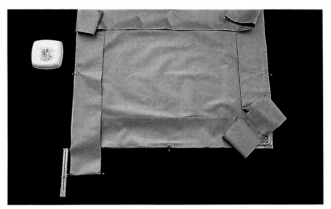

12) Align notches on one flange with notches on sham at center of each side. Seamlines of flange will be at opposite corners. Mark corners of flange with pins. Repeat for remaining flange.

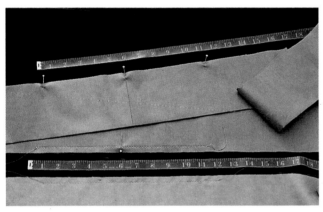

13) Zigzag over heavy thread on the wrong side of each flange, beginning and ending 5½" (14 cm) on either side of corner pins. Leave 3" (7.5 cm) thread tails at each end.

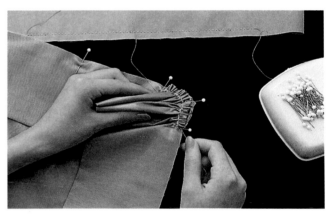

14) Pin narrow flange to front, matching notches. Draw up gathers so flange fits sham front. Wrap threads around pins to secure; machine-baste at corners only. Place wide flange over narrow flange; gather and pin.

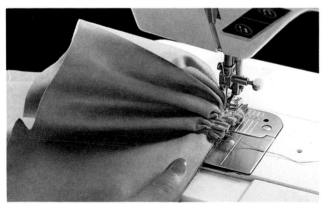

15) Machine-baste through all layers ⅜" (1 cm) from raw edge, using zipper foot. Pound the layers with a hammer to flatten before stitching, if necessary.

16) Place sham front and back right sides together, with front on top; pin. Stitch around sham ½" (1.3 cm) from edge. Serge or zigzag raw edges. Turn right side out; steam gathers. Insert pillow.

Slipcovers for Folding Chairs

Slipcovers for folding chairs are an easy and affordable way to dress up an old steel folding chair. For special occasions, for a change of seasons, or simply for some fun in home decorating, folding-chair slipcovers are attractive and versatile. They can work with any decorating scheme from contemporary to country, depending upon fabric choice and styling options. And they offer a practical solution to the age-old problem posed by large gatherings: attractive yet portable and stowable temporary seating.

Folding chairs come in a variety of shapes and sizes, quite similar but not exactly the same. To make a well-fitting slipcover, make a custom-fitted pattern out of muslin. Start with four rectangles of fabric cut approximately to size, then drape and pin them to the chair to fine-tune the shape. Once this muslin has been fitted, use it as a pattern for cutting the slipcover.

When you make the actual slipcover, add a decorative bow tied across the back, or add contrasting piping or ruffles or creative touches of your own.

YOU WILL NEED

3 yd. (2.75 m) unbleached muslin, 42" (107 cm) wide, for pattern.

Folding chair.

Marker or pencil, pins, shears, double-stick tape.

Heavy weight, such as books or gallon (3.78 L) bottle of water.

Decorator fabric.

Muslin pattern layout. Mark muslin for rough pattern pieces; cut on solid lines. Mark dotted center lines. Mark arrows on skirt pattern piece, 6" (15 cm) and 12" (30.5 cm) on each side of center line.

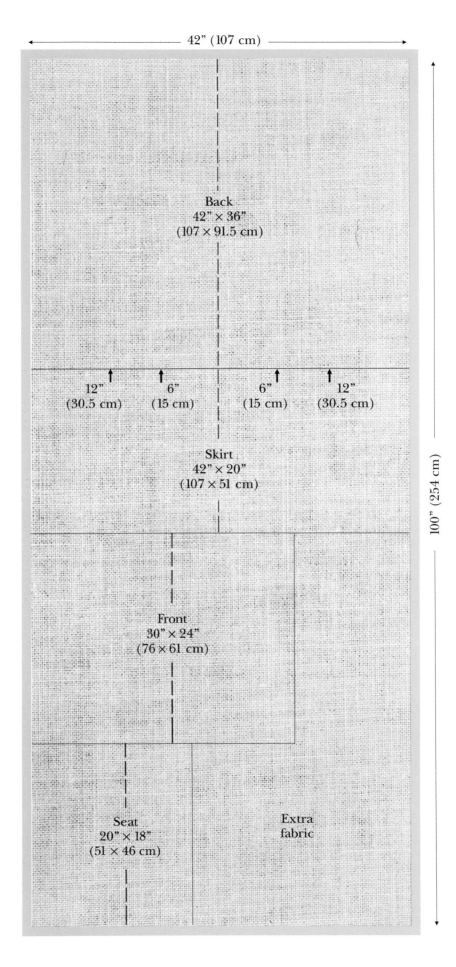

42" (107 cm)

Back
42" × 36"
(107 × 91.5 cm)

12"
(30.5 cm)   6"
(15 cm)   6"
(15 cm)   12"
(30.5 cm)

Skirt
42" × 20"
(107 × 51 cm)

Front
30" × 24"
(76 × 61 cm)

Seat
20" × 18"
(51 × 46 cm)

Extra
fabric

100" (254 cm)

How to Make a Folding Chair Slipcover

1) **Pin** back and front pattern pieces together for 4" (10 cm) on either side of the center marks. Pin horizontally from center toward sides, using a ½" (1.3 cm) seam allowance.

2) **Drape** pinned pattern over chair, matching center lines to center of chair back. Secure pattern at top of chair back with double-stick tape. Tuck pattern under back legs; keep grainline straight.

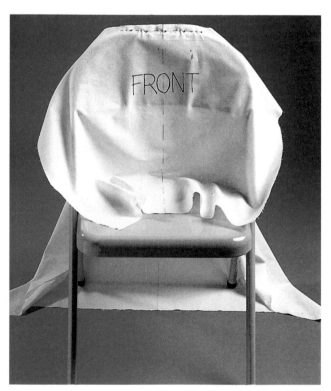

3) **Push** front pattern piece toward back edge of seat at bottom to allow enough ease for sitting. Secure pattern to chair with double-stick tape at center of seat and both corners.

4) **Drape** back pattern around curve of chair. Drape smoothly, keeping grainline perpendicular to floor. Pin along edge of chair to indicate seamline. Repeat for other side.

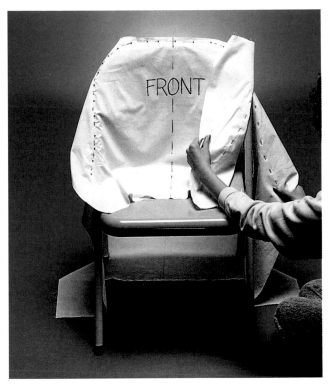

5) Drape front pattern around curve of chair. Pin along edge of chair to indicate seamline. Pin back pattern to front pattern along seamlines, adjusting to fit chair smoothly and maintain grainline.

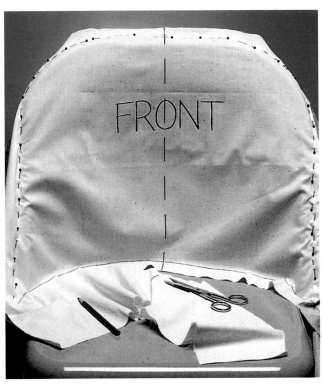

6) Trace edge of the chair seat at bottom of front pattern. Trim to 1" (2.5 cm) beyond traced outline.

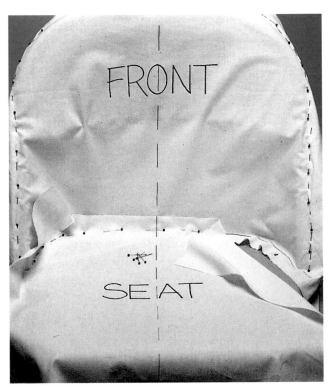

7) Secure seat pattern to chair at center front with double-stick tape. Pin back of seat pattern to bottom of front pattern, stopping where the front and back pieces meet.

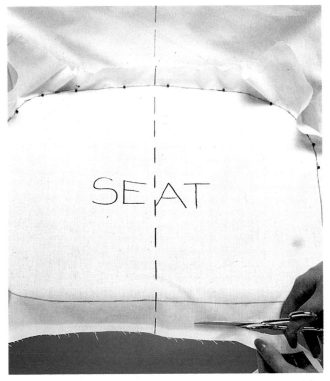

8) Trace outline of chair seat onto seat pattern. Add ¼" (6 mm) to front edge of seat pattern to allow for the rounded front edge of chair. Trim to 1" (2.5 cm) beyond outline.

(Continued on next page)

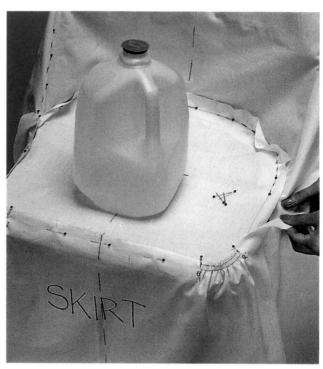

9) Gather or pleat skirt pattern between 6" and 12" (15 and 30.5 cm) marks on each side of center line. Draw up each set of gathers to 3" (7.5 cm).

10) Weight pattern pieces on chair so they do not move; a gallon (3.78 L) of water or stack of books works well. Match center lines of seat and skirt patterns. Pin skirt to seat ending where all four pieces meet.

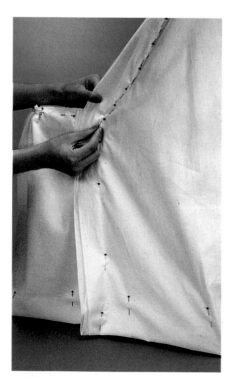

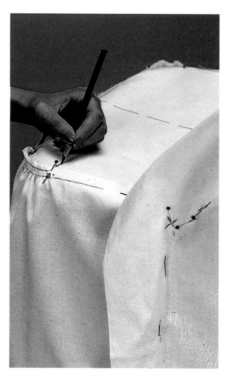

11) Turn up and pin hem to the desired length. Pin skirt to back pattern at sides. Examine fit of muslin on chair and make any necessary adjustments. Pattern should fit snugly, without pulling.

12) Mark seamlines between pins on all pieces. Mark placement for gathers on seat and skirt patterns. Mark all pieces with an "X" at point where all four pattern pieces meet at sides.

13) Remove pins and release gathers. Lay pieces flat. Mark seamlines. Fold pieces along centers. Compare markings on each half. Make any necessary adjustments so pattern is symmetrical.

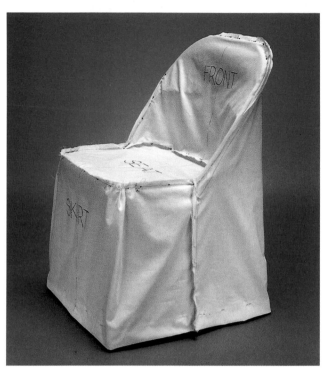

14) Trim hem allowance on skirt to 2" (5 cm) for a finished 1" (2.5 cm) double-fold hem.

15) Repin, and try pattern on chair. Adjust the fit, seamlines, and placement marks, as necessary. Add ½" (1.3 cm) seam allowances; trim excess fabric. Try pattern on chair again, if desired.

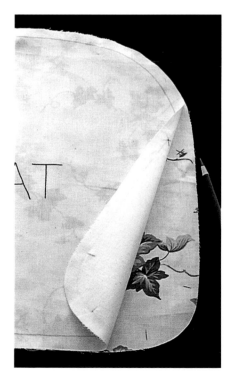

16) Cut chair cover from decorator fabric, using the muslin pieces as a pattern. Transfer markings.

17) Cut two pieces for ties, each 7" (18 cm) wide and 42" (107 cm) long. Fold in half lengthwise, right sides together. Fold one end to form triangle; cut on fold. Stitch cut side and bias end; turn and press.

18) Stitch front to seat along back edge of seat between Xs **(a).** Stitch back to skirt at side seams, inserting tie in seam **(b).** Gather skirt between markings; stitch front/seat to back/skirt **(c).** Stitch hem.

Reverse Roll-up Shade

The reverse roll-up shade is a practical shade, covering the window frame and hanging from a self-lined valance. The contrasting lining that rolls to the outside of the shade is fused to the shade fabric.

Select two mediumweight, firmly woven fabrics that will bond well. Do not use fabrics that are water-resistant and stain-resistant. Such fabrics are treated with silicone, which prevents bonding. Test a sample to be sure the fabrics bond securely. To prevent pattern show-through when sunlight comes through the shade, use a solid-colored lining; light colors will also show sun fading less than strong colors.

Determine the placement of the mounting board before taking measurements. If the shade is more than 36" (91.5 cm) wide, an angle iron needs to be added at the center of the mounting board. This may make it necessary to mount the shade higher above the window. The reverse roll-up shade goes to the sill, but because the lining is decorative, a portion of the shade is always rolled to the right side, even when the shade is lowered.

✂ Cutting Directions

Cut shade fabric and fusible web 1" (2.5 cm) wider than outside window measurement and 12" (30.5 cm) longer than length from mounting board to sill. Cut lining 2" (5 cm) wider and 1½" (3.8 cm) longer than shade fabric. Cut two lengths of shade cord, 3 times the length of the shade plus width.

YOU WILL NEED

Shade fabric, contrasting solid lining, valance fabric, and fusible web.

Mounting board, 1" × 4" (2.5 × 10 cm) lumber, 4" (10 cm) wider than finished shade.

Four screw eyes, ½" (1.3 cm).

Two 2" (5 cm) angle irons and screws for mounting.

Cardboard upholsterer's stripping, width of finished shade.

One dowel, ½" (1.3 cm), width of finished shade.

Shade cord; awning cleat; drapery pull.

Note: If shade is wider than 36" (91.5 cm), add another angle iron, shade cord, and two screw eyes.

How to Make a Reverse Roll-up Shade and Valance

1) Place lining *wrong* side up on large padded surface. Center the fusible web from side to side, even with the top and 1½" (3.8 cm) from the bottom.

2) Place shade fabric *right* side up on lining, aligning edges with the fusible web. Fuse shade fabric to lining, following manufacturer's directions.

3) Serge or stitch top edge. Press lining to right side in double ½" (1.3 cm) side hems; stitch. Press ½" (1.3 cm), then 1" (2.5 cm) to right side on lower edge; stitch.

4) Insert dowel in lower rod pocket.

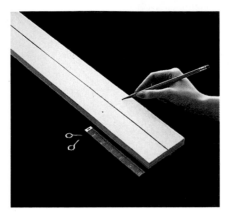

5) Draw line lengthwise down the center of mounting board, and mark position of screw eyes 1" (2.5 cm) in front of and behind marked line and 6" (15 cm) from ends of mounting board. Drill 4 holes for screw eyes.

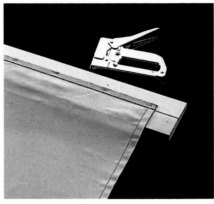

6) Center top shade lengthwise on board and ⅜" (1 cm) above marked line. Place the cardboard stripping along top edge of shade; staple.

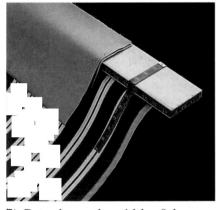

7) Cut valance the width of the mounting board and ends plus 1" (2.5 cm) for seam allowances; cut length twice the length from back of the mounting board to desired lower edge.

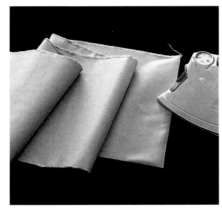

8) Fold fabric in half lengthwise, right sides together, and stitch ½" (1.3 cm) seams on each end. Turn, press, and serge or zigzag raw edges together.

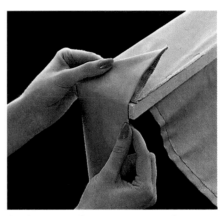

9) Center valance on mounting board; staple along back side. Wrap valance around ends of mounting board. Miter the corners on top of board; staple in place.

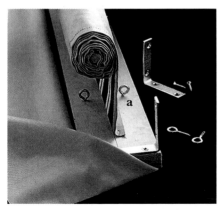

10) Insert screw eyes into drilled holes; add angle iron on each end of mounting board. Tie cord to screw eye **(a)** at back of board.

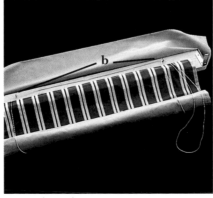

11) Loop cord around shade, and thread through screw eye **(b)** at front. Repeat for second side. Bring one cord across the top and thread through front screw eye on pull side.

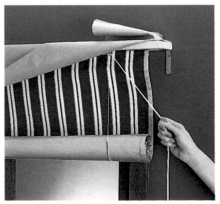

12) Mount the valance and shade. Adjust cord so shade is level and at the desired full length; tie knot at front right screw eye. Add drapery pull, if desired.

Index

Buckles, covering, 102
Buttonholes, 10
Buttons, 10

C

Cable stitch, for smocking, 77-79
Carrageenan, for marbling fabric, 41-42
Chairs, folding, slipcovers for, 97, 119-123
Channel-stitched cuffs, 18-19
Chevroned bias sleeves, 16-17
Christmas ornament, smocked, 81-82
Clustered gathers, on bed
  skirts, 97, 111-113
Color,
  for dyeing fabric, 32-33
  for quilting, 72
Comforter covers, from
  sheets, 97, 107-109
Copying design details, 12-13
Couture details, on sleeves, 14-19
Covered belt buckles, 102
Covered shoulder pads, 14-15
Creative details,
  see: design details, lace,
  ruching, sleeves
Creative lace, 44-47
Cuffs, channel-stitched, 18-19
Cutting on the bias, 16-17

D

Decorative openings, for heirloom
  fabric, 50
Design, surface, 58-59
  also see: specific techniques
Design details, 10-11
  copying, 12-13
Designing a quilt, 72-75
Direct application method, for
  tie-dyeing, 37-39
Double-flange pillow shams, 97, 114-117
Double-wing needles, for special
  effects, 52-54
Duvet covers, from sheets, 97, 107-109
Dyeing,
  fabric, 30-35
  lace, 47

E

Edging lace, for heirloom fabric, 48, 51
Embellishments, surface, 58-59
  also see: specific techniques
Embroidery, 66-67
English smocking, 76-79
Entredeux, for heirloom fabric, 48, 50
Even Feed™ foot 53, 57

A

Accessories,
  also see: specific items
  creative, 96
  for special effects, 53, 56-57
Applied ruches, 22-24
Appliqué, 66-67
  hand, for quilting, 90-93
  hemstitched insert, 55

B

Baskets, rag, 84-86
Battenberg lace, creating by
  machine, 20-21
Beading, 66-67
Beading lace, for heirloom fabric, 48
Bed skirts, with clustered
  gathers, 97, 111-113
Belt buckles, covering, 102
Belts, designer, 96, 102-103
Bias-cut sleeves, 16-17
Block rotation, for quilting, 74-75
Blooming, in slashing, 58, 65
Box-pleated ruches, 22-24
Braided rug, 87-89

F

Fabric,
  creating hand-dyed, 30-35
  marbling, 41-43
  painting, 66
  tie-dyeing, 36-40
Fabric loops, as buttonholes, 10
Feet, special-purpose, for special
  effect, 53-57
Fiber-reactive dyes, 30, 34, 37
Folding chairs, slipcovers for, 97, 119-123
French hand sewing, to create heirloom
  fabric, 48-51

G

Garment sections, ruched, 22, 25
Gathered inset ruches, 23, 26
Gathering foot, 53, 56-57
Gathers, clustered, on bed
  skirts, 97, 111-113
Glasses case, smocked, 83

H

Hand appliqué, for quilting, 90-93
Handbags, 96, 98-101
Hand-braided rug, 87-89
Hand-dyed fabric, 30-35
  marbling, 41-43
  tie-dyeing, 36-40
Heart appliqué, for quilting, 91-93
Heirloom fabric, creating, 48-51
Heirloom trims, 50-51
Hemstitching, 52, 54-55
Home, creative projects for, 96-97
  also see: specific items

I

Immersion method, for tie-dyeing, 36-38
Insertion lace, for heirloom fabric, 48, 51
Inset ruches, 23, 26-27
Insets, on handbags, 96, 98-99, 101

L

Lace,
  applying, 21
  beading, for heirloom fabric, 48
  creating by machine, 20-21
  creative, 44-47
  dyeing, 47
  edging, for heirloom fabric, 48, 51
  insertion, for heirloom fabric, 48, 51

sewing, 45
Leather trims, 10-11
Loops, fabric, as buttonholes, 10

M

Marbling fabric, 41-43
Muffler, wool, 104-105

N

Needles, wing, for special
   effects, 52-55

O

Ornament, smocked Christmas, 81-82
Oval braided rug, 88-89

P

Painting fabric, 66
Patchwork, Seminole, 62
Patterns,
   for duplicating designer details, 13
   for tie-dyeing, 36-39
Piecing, 60-61
Pillow shams, double-flange, 97, 114-117
Pin tucks, 56-57
   for heirloom fabric, 50
Pin-tuck foot, 50, 53, 56-57
Piping, 11
Plaid pattern, for tie-dyeing, 39
Pleating, 63
Pleating machine, for smocking, 76-77
Prairie points, in piecing, 60
Procion® dye, 30, 34, 37
Puff paints, 66
Puffing strips, for heirloom fabric, 48, 51

Q

Quilt top, appliqué, 90-93
Quilting, color and design, 72-75

R

Rag baskets, 84-86
Reverse roll-up shades, 97, 124-125

Ribbon twists, for heirloom fabric, 50
Roll-up shades, reverse, 97, 124-125
Roll-up sleeves, 11
Ruching, 22-27
Rug braiding, 87-89

S

Satin stitch foot, 53
Scarves, 96, 104-105
Seminole patchwork, 62
Sewing,
   on the bias, 16
   lace, tips for, 45
   ruches, tips for, 23
Shades, reverse roll-up, 97, 124-125
Shams, pillow, double-flange, 97, 114-117
Shaped center seams, on sleeves, 14-15
Sheets, for comforter covers, 97, 107-109
Shine and sparkle, adding, 68-69
Shoulder pads, covered, 14-15
Single-wing needles, for special
   effects, 52-55
Slashing, 58, 65
Sleeves,
   bias-cut, 16-17
   details on, 14-19
   roll-up, 11
Slipcovers, for folding chairs, 97, 119-123
Smocked Christmas ornament, 81-82
Smocking,
   English, 76-79
   projects, 83
Snail-shirred ruches, 22, 24
Snakeskin, for belt buckles, 102
Special effects, 52-55
   accessories for, 56-57
Special-purpose feet, for special
   effects, 53-57
Starburst pattern, for tie-dyeing, 36-37
Stitching,
   cable, for smocking, 77-79
   channel, on cuffs, 18-19
   hem-, 52, 54-55
   trellis, 77-79
Striped pattern, for tie-dyeing, 36, 38
Strips, puffing, for heirloom
   fabric, 48, 51
Suede trims, 10-11
Surface design, 58-59
   also see: specific techniques
Synthetic suede,
   belts, 102-103
   handbags, 98-101
Synthrapol®, 30, 34-35, 37

T

Tieback, smocked, 83
Tie-dyeing, 36-40
Trellis stitch, 77-79

Triangle-tipped inset ruches, 23, 27
Trimmings, 10-11
Trims, heirloom, 50-51
Twists, ribbon, for heirloom fabric, 50

U

Ultrasuede®, 10
   also see: synthetic suede

W

Wing needles, for special
   effects, 50, 52-55
Wool muffler, 104-105

Cy DeCosse Incorporated offers
sewing accessories to subscribers.
For information write:
   Sewing Accessories
   5900 Green Oak Drive
   Minnetonka, MN 55343